Jon Spoelstra
Wall Street Journal Bestselling Author

Pigs-that-Fly
HACK

A Business Fable of
Wonderful Destinies

A self-help success hack to create
ideas when and where
you need them most

Pigs That Fly Hack

This self-help success hack to create ideas
when and where you need them most

A Business Fable of Wonderful Destinies

Idea Series #1: Creating

Wall Street Journal Best Selling Author
Jon Spoelstra

"I just thought Jon's ideas just came to him. Like poof! Now I understand this magical guru of ideas actually had an idea plan, committed to practice and then a stalwart defense of that idea."
Buffy Filippell
Founder, Teamwork Online

"I have had the good fortune to work with some of the best and brightest minds in the sports and entertainment business. By far, the brightest mind, the most entrepreneurial leader and thinker is Jon. He is brilliant at ideas, but even better at converting them into reality."
Tim Leiweke
CEO, Oak View Group

"I remember seeing many of the creative ideas Jon brought to life over the years. I often wondered first, 'How did he think of that?' Now I know. I wish I'd had this info 40 years ago."
Steve Patterson
President, Pro Sports Consulting

"This is like a master magician showing you step-by-step how to do his most famous magic trick, but this is better—you learn the secret on how to get your boss to approve whatever you want to do."
Joe Sugarman
Chairman, BluBlocker Sunglasses

"One can't believe impossible things."

"I daresay you haven't had much practice," said the Queen. "When I was your age, I always did it for half an hour a day. Why, sometimes I believed in as many as six impossible things before breakfast."
                               Lewis Carroll, *Alice in Wonderland*

I'm thankful I had a system that regularly created timely ideas that boosted me at each step of my career. That system is in this book. Use it. Enjoy.
                               Jon Spoelstra, *Pigs That Fly Hack*

Copyright 2021 by Jon Spoelstra
ISBN 9798536336915

All rights reserved. Excerpt as permitted under the U.S. Copyright Act of 1976, no part of this publication may be reproduced, distributed, or transmitted in any form or by any means or stored in a database or retrieval system, without the prior written permission of the author.

Author's Foreword

Jon Spoelstra

What's this about flying pigs?

I owe the flying pigs to some of my former bosses.

While many of my ideas might be considered mundane (but were highly useful in advancing my career), some ideas were way out there. One such idea led my boss to say, "That'll work when pigs fly." Of course, the idea did indeed work.

That idea didn't just float through the air and lodge somewhere in my brain, eventually popping up in my consciousness. Nope, it was a 'manufactured' idea.

Most of my ideas were created through *a process*. No magic here; these ideas are *human made*. In other words, they are *manufactured*.

To manufacture these ideas, I used the coolest hack. That's right, a *shortcut to impactful ideas*. It's sorta been my secret. I've been using it for a long, long time.

I sat down and wrote how to use this hack to create those human-made ideas. To make it more fun, I wrote it in the style of a business fable. You read that right—a *fable*. It's just a lot more fun for me—and most likely you—to divulge my secret hack this way.

It will take you about an hour to read it and fully understand the system. Is it worth it? Well, what's *one* great idea worth to you? What are *a lot of great ideas* worth to you? How about a *lifetime* of ideas that continually enhance your career?

Jon

P.S. You'll find that the ideas you cherish are the 'flying pig ideas.' When your boss says, "That'll work when pigs fly," you'll know you've got a terrific breakthrough idea.

So, start the process. Start manufacturing ideas, today. You'll have fun.

Chapter 1

DISCLAIMER: MUST READ BEFORE PROCEEDING

This is the most unusual—maybe even wacky—story that you have ever heard. Ever.

Even though you may disbelieve parts of it or even lots of it, I ask just one favor: Suspend your disbelief for only a short while.

Go ahead, pretend you're a kid again, and put your disbelief to rest. If you do, this story will have a profound effect on you. How so? In a nutshell, your life might never again be the same.

My story starts simply enough. It starts with an aerosol can.
On an Oregon beach.

The beaches in Oregon are the best walking beaches in the world. When it's low tide, the water will recede up to a hundred yards, leaving hard-packed sand. If you wanted to string up a net, the surface would be tournament-ready for playing tennis.

When you walk close to the waves, you can find all kinds of neat shells just lying there on the hard sand. Like Sand Dollars. And, occasionally, a Chinaman's Cap, a small shell that does look like…well…a Chinaman's cap.

In the winter, you can walk for miles and not see anybody.

The weather's not bad—usually in the 40s—and the scenery is terrific with huge rock outcroppings, forests and the blustery sea. If you ever wanted to just walk and think, think and walk, this is the place.

Haystack Rock is a landmark at Cannon Beach, and during some winter days, it would be only you and Haystack on the beach.

Walking with my head down, scanning the sand, I saw an aerosol can. There's not a lot of litter on the beach—I think the ocean sort of sucks that stuff up and somehow distributes it to a San Francisco beach or someplace like that—so seeing the can was unusual. Even more unusual were the words on it. They were in Japanese.

The Japanese characters made this different than your average litter. Heck, this piece of trash might have even floated the seven thousand miles from Japan!

I picked it up. I couldn't read a word of Japanese. But it seemed to be an aerosol can of paint. I couldn't tell what color. I decided to give it a try to see if the color was blue or maybe some exotic fluorescent color.

I pressed the nozzle.

Nothing happened.

I pressed again. Nothing.

Then I felt movement inside the aerosol can. It felt like a frog thrashing to get out. Whirling and bumping and jumping. Just as I was going to drop the can on the sand, an explosion of smoke and mist fired out of the nozzle. That's when I first met my genie.

From that point on, my life changed more than you could imagine. This is the first time I've ever told anybody about this. Who wants to get labeled as stark raving crazy like those loonies who claim UFOs abducted them or those folks who swear they've seen Bigfoot? Not me. I got enough problems.

There are folks that can explain UFOs, I think. The same for Bigfoot. But *a genie in an aerosol can*? No way! That's so off the wall it would be too bizarre even for the tabloids. And, it is so outrageous, I might lose *you* here. *Yeah, sure, a genie,* you're probably saying to yourself. But hold on: remember the DISCLAIMER at the beginning of this book where, I assume, you agreed to suspend your disbelief for a short time. Again, I ask you, just suspend your disbelief for the moment. Later on, you'll thank me. You might even write me into your will.

This genie wasn't like a scantily clad Barbara Eden in *I Dream of Jeannie*. The genie that came out of the spray can was big. I'd say about six foot three, weighing maybe 250 pounds, at least. And *Japanese*. In size, he reminded me of a Japanese Dick Butkus. In looks, his cousin could have been Oddjob, the henchman in the James Bond movie *Goldfinger*. Still, he looked stylish, wearing what appeared to be a gray pinstripe Italian suit. Those Japanese always know good fashion.

You might think I was hallucinating. Heck, if I had had time to think, *I* would have thought I was hallucinating. But this happened so quickly, I just stood there staring at this big genie.

"*Arigato gozaimasu*," he said. I stared at him.

He probably could tell I didn't understand a word. "Thank you very much," he said, translating for me.

I was regaining some composure. You know how sometimes you think of a zillion things in about a nanosecond? That's the way my mind was racing now. My brain examined and discarded everything from the possibility of hallucination to insanity to a combination of both. I tossed the thought that the triple-pepperoni pizza I had last night could have caused this insanity—it had never caused those side effects before.

Darrell had an uncanny likeness to that character Odd Job in the James Bond movie Goldfinger.

Before I could explore more in a second nanosecond, the big genie spoke again.

"I'm Darrell," he said, extending a hand for me to shake.

I reached out and shook it. It was *real flesh*. This guy was not one of those apparitions you could see through. He was the real McCoy, even though he did somehow burst out of an aerosol can.

"Darrell?" I asked.

That wasn't a Japanese name.

As if reading my thoughts, he said, "My real name is Yoshifumi, but I wanted to Americanize it for you."

Darrell? Maybe he wanted to prove to me he could handle the r's and the l's. He did flawlessly.

"You're Elmer, right?" he asked.

I nodded. Just as I was about to ask how he knew my name, he thrust his big right hand out to shake mine and said, "Good to meet yah."

"What are you?" I asked, sort of blurting it out.

"Just what you thought I was when I came flying out of that aerosol can. A genie." Then he pulled open his suit coat and showed the Armani label. "Just a little more modern." Strangely, he spoke with a strong Brooklyn accent.

5

"So, pal," he said, "let's get on with it. You've got two wishes."

"I thought the deal was three wishes," I said.

"Ahh, you Americans. You always exaggerate, exaggerate, exaggerate. *Bigger! More!* Well, lemme tell you, pal, it has *always* been two wishes, always *will* be two wishes. So, what's it gonna be?"

I laughed. This whole thing was too crazy. Maybe triple-pepperoni pizza does make you hallucinate. OK, I thought, since I'm here and since this guy appears to be a genie, I'll just play along with my hallucination until reality fades in.

"My first wish," I said, rolling my eyes skyward, giving the appearance of thinking, "is that I want to have *three* wishes."

"A wise guy, eh?" he said. "This ain't no joking matter. In fact, I'm sad to say, Elmer, I'm not going to grant you your first wish. And you forfeit that wish for being a wise guy."

Darrell sure didn't have much of a sense of humor.

"You're kidding, of course," I said.

"Nope. That's it, Elmer. *One wish*. Take it or leave it."

He picked up the aerosol can and tossed it in his hand. "C'mon, let's take a walk. I'd like to stretch my legs." Off he went. I caught up to him and hustled to stay in lockstep, stride for stride.

"There are some things that you can't wish for," he said casually.

"I didn't realize there were ground rules," I said.

"Oh yeah, what d'ya think this is winning the lottery or something?" Darrell asked.

"Well, now that you mention it, yes."

"Nope. Not at all. Here are the ground rules, pal."

Darrell stopped and turned toward the ocean. "Beautiful, isn't it? Wow! I've been in that can a long time."

"The ground rules?" I reminded him.

"Oh yeah. The first ground rule is that you can't ask for money."

"You can't?" I asked.

"Don't look so disappointed, pal," Darrell said. "That's why this isn't like winning the lottery. If you want money, go work for some crazy Internet company and hope they take it public. Or, merge a company with your competitor. The Wall Street folks will love you, and you can cash out your stock a little while later and make a fortune. But don't worry about the money as far as your wish is concerned. If you wish the right thing, the money will naturally take care of itself."

That was easy for him to say. I don't think he needed any money. After all, Darrell was a genie. He could just wish for things, and they would come true. Like that Armani suit he was wearing. I can't imagine him sauntering into a fancy men's store in New York City and plunking down three or four grand in cash for a suit when he could blink it on.

For me, money hasn't been that easy. Sure, I make a decent living as a real estate agent. But you aren't going to see me buying any major league sports team, or minor league team for that matter. Heck, I really can't afford season tickets in the nose-bleed seats to Blazer games even though I have them. Each year it seems I have to sell off more tickets to friends. I've even gone to the extreme of advertising on Craigslist and Facebook to sell some of my tickets to strangers. There are 41 home games; I sell off about 35 or 36. So, it looks like *my* season ticket is five or six lousy games.

While I was thinking how unfair this ground rule was, the genie said, "There's a second ground rule."

I looked up at him.

"No women."

"No women? What do you mean?"

"Well, some guys would ask for some movie star to fall in love with them," Darrell said. "You know, a beautiful, rich and famous movie star becoming your love slave. Women aren't a part of the deal. You have to work that out for yourself. I'm a *business* genie—I'm a *specialist*."

Terrific, that's just terrific. I run across a genie, and he can't provide me money or women.

The women part wasn't so bad. I'm married. Although we seemed to have hit a few speed bumps somewhere along the way. That's why I played hooky from work today and drove out to this lonely Oregon beach. I was thinking and walking and wondering why my life and my marriage were on a slow treadmill. While Darrell was explaining the second ground rule, I have to admit that another flash of thoughts appeared in a nanosecond—thoughts forged in the fantasy of wishing for some rich and famous movie star to fall in love with me. For just that nanosecond, it seemed pretty appealing and exciting.

"Anyplace around here we can get something to eat?" Darrell asked.

I told him there was a place to eat about a half-mile up the beach.

"Let's go, I'm starved," Darrell said, picking up the pace. He walked as quietly as a ghost.

"Oh, by the way, you've got a week to come up with your wish," Darrell said.

Chapter 2

Lewis and Clark carved out The Oregon Trail in the 1850s.
They led their wagon train over plains that had no interstate highways.

Somehow they got their wagons around and over mountains that would intimidate most of today's skiers.

They forded gushing rivers that had salmon the size of dogs leaping upstream.

They fought off Indians who didn't know they were trying to protect their land for future casinos.

And finally, after twenty-eight months of this stuff, they ended up looking the Pacific Ocean right in the eye. Of course, one sighting never written up in the history books was when they first saw Bill's Tavern.

"What's that?" Lewis asked Clark, pointing south down the beach.

"It must be a mirage," Clark said, squinting, then rubbing his eyes. "We've been traveling for way too many months. Yeah, it's a mirage."

They were looking at a plank building. The words painted on the side read: Bill's Tavern *Fresh Draft Beer.*

If Lewis and Clark walked into this mirage, they would have seen a bar with unemployed loggers.

Sure, I'm exaggerating a bit about how long Bill's Tavern has been there, but it seems like it has been there forever.

That's where I took Darrell.

Two old guys were sitting at the bar. They looked old enough to have had a beer or two with Meriwether Lewis and William Clark. Strangely, this version of Bill's Tavern wasn't the new one. A few years ago, the owners had rebuilt Bill's Tavern in its original location. This rebuilt version looked like it could double as an ice cream parlor that catered to tourists. Bright and cheery. The bar that Darrell and I walked into was the original, dark one, and the floor creaked as we stepped across the floor to an open booth. If you looked closely enough at the floor, you could spot some ancient bloodstains from a time long ago when men were men, and a fight was just good Friday night entertainment. That was, of course, before cable, ESPN and Netflix.

The menu at Bill's was limited. Clam chowder. Cheeseburger with potato chips. A ham sandwich. Chili. Take it or leave. When they rebuilt the joint, they added a brewpub with a lot of fancy beers, but today it was either Guinness or Bud on tap.

The cheeseburgers were the best in the world. Don't even think about the fat content being about seventy percent. Think about the taste! And while you're at it, throw a couple strips of bacon on it.

The two guys at the bar glanced at Darrell. It's not too often they see a six-foot-three inch, 250-pound Japanese guy dressed up like a fancy Italian. They were so focused on Darrell that I don't think they even saw me.

A scrawny guy with a ponytail walked over to our table. He was a former unemployed lumberjack and was now the bartender, waiter, and cook. "What'll it be, fellas?" he asked.

Darrell didn't have to think. "A bowl of clam chowder, a bowl of chili, four cheeseburgers, two pints of Guinness," he said.

The bartender-waiter-cook nodded and turned to walk away.

"Wait a minute," Darrell said. "How about my friend?"

"I thought your order was for both of you."

Darrell said, "Nope."

The waiter looked at me. I said, "Cheeseburger and a pint of Bud for me."

Moments later, the bartender delivered the beer, and Darrell snatched it before the glass reached the tabletop. It was a pretty nifty handoff from the bartender to Darrell. Darrell raised the beer in a salute to me, or God knows who. I raised mine and did likewise. "To one wish," Darrell said. I nodded.

"So, pal, what do you do for a living?" Darrell asked.

"Why do you talk that way?" I asked, changing the subject.

"What way?"

"You know, you talk like you're from Brooklyn. *Pal* this, *pal* that. I know you didn't come from Brooklyn."

Darrell laughed. "I just like the sound of it. I speak 118 languages, but the one I like the best is Brooklynese."

"That's not a language, Darrell, that's an accent."

"So, sue me, pal. Now, Elmer, what do you do for a living?"

"Real estate," I said.

"Invest? Commercial? Houses? What?"

"I'm just a real estate salesman—houses." I said.

"How do you like it?" Darrell asked.

I shrugged. "It's a living."

The foam on Darrell's Guinness was settling down, and he took a long swallow.

"Probably not too successful," he said, some of the foam on his lip.

"As I said, it's a living," I said.

"Well, there are three ways to the top in any business," he said. "This is true throughout the world. Always has been, always will be."

I took a long swallow from my Bud. Here was my genie with a Brooklyn accent pontificating about life! What does he know about life? He's been in a can of spray paint.

"Elmer, is your father still alive?" he asked.

I nodded.

"Is he rich? Does he own his own business? Is it a *big* business?"

"No to each of those questions," I said. I drank some more Bud. The way I was cranking through this one, maybe I should have ordered two at a time like Darrell.

"That's too bad. That's the first way to the top. *Inherit* it. That's the best way—*inherit* it," Darrell said. "I know, some will say that if you inherit a fortune it will deprive you of the *opportunity* of earning and doing. That may be true, but if you had indeed inherited a fortune, you wouldn't be walking the beach alone. You'd have a huge house on the beach, and you'd be walking with your mistress. Not bad, eh? But it doesn't sound like this is your path to the top. How about your wife? She rich?"

"Nope."

"That's too bad, Elmer. That's the second way to the top. *Marry* into it."

Darrell drained his first Guinness and started on his second. He sighed.

"OK, Darrell, you've got me going oh-for-two," I said. "I didn't inherit it, and I didn't marry into it. What's the third way to the top?"

"Do you have a mentor? You know, somebody that you respect that guides you when making important decisions?"

I shook my head, no.

"Well, that's not so bad. Mentors are overrated as far as I am concerned. Sure, they can give you advice and make a few introductions for you, maybe give you a few shortcuts, but then you still gotta do it yourself anyway."

The ponytailed bartender brought over the bowl of clam chowder and the bowl of chili and placed them in front of Darrell. Darrell took alternating slurps from his chowder and chili.

"Your boss a good guy?" he asked me.

"He's a jerk," I said, watching some chowder slide out of Darrell's mouth. "A real jerk."

"Well, that's OK too," Darrell said. "It would be better if you learned a lot from your boss; if he was an inspiration to you; if you respected him; if you liked him. But that's OK."

"What's OK about it?" I asked.

"The third way to the top. *Ride the right horse*. The right horse *could* be a powerful mentor. The right horse *could* be an inspiring boss. But when it's all said and done, the right horse has to be *you. Ride the right horse.* Ride *yourself.*"

Yeah, sure, I thought, ride the right horse. Ride *me*! Ha! That was so stupid! The way I was going, I was riding myself right into a life so dull that if you assigned a color to it, it would be a muddy *gray*.

Chapter 3

Have you ever seen a guy eat four greasy—deliciously so—cheeseburgers at one sitting? I hadn't either, until Darrell. Interestingly, he didn't eat them one at a time. I don't mean that he tried to eat all four at the same time. Instead, he took a bite out of one. "*Hmmmmmmm,*" he said. Then he took a bite out of another. "*Hmmmmmmm, good.*" Then a bite out of the third. Then the fourth. It's like he was alternating between steak and lobster and vegetables. Except, he was alternating between cheeseburger, cheeseburger, cheeseburger, and cheeseburger. Yup, strange guy. Or, I guess you'd say, strange *genie*.

The process continued until he had finished all the burgers. While he was eating, Darrell wasn't talking except for the occasional *hmmmmmmm*.

The two old guys at the bar seemed impressed with Darrell. Not with his quirky eating style —I don't think these guys were into style points for eating—but with the volume. They probably figured he was one of those sumo wrestling guys.

While the last bite was in his mouth, Darrell said, "I'll be with you for the week."

"What do you mean?"

"Well, you've got a big decision to make," Darrell said, wiping his mouth with a paper napkin. "You might need some advice from someone who has experience in this type of stuff. That's me, pal. Nobody's more of an expert on wishes than me. So, wherever you go, I go."

He could tell that I was mulling this over.

"Don't worry," he said, "I won't get in the way. Trust me, nobody will notice me. Here, let me give you a little demonstration."

The ponytailed waiter arrived at the table to clear the dishes. "Anything else?" he asked.

I said, "Cup of coffee."

"What about your friend?" the waiter asked. I looked at Darrell. He just sat there smiling like a huge Japanese Cheshire cat.

"Ask him," I said, "He speaks English."

"Where did he go?" The waiter asked.

"He's right there," I said, pointing at Darrell.

The waiter looked at me as if I was hallucinating from some freako recipe of drugs and cheeseburgers. Darrell kept smiling at me.

"I'll make some fresh coffee. It'll be a few minutes," the waiter said to me and walked back to the bar, mumbling to himself.

"See?" Darrell said.

"See what?" I replied.

"That's the point. The waiter didn't *see* me. He thinks you're some whacko, by the way."

"You can make yourself *invisible*?" I asked.

Darrell nodded, smiling. "Among other truly amazing and astounding things. I can turn it on and off like a faucet. I'd be a great act out in Las Vegas."

"Or bank robbing."

Darrell chuckled.

"It's a little trick I learned from Einstein, the disappearing," Darrell said.

"From *Albert* Einstein?"

"Who else? You think it would be *Ralph* Einstein?" Darrell asked. "Yep, old Albert was famous for developing the Theory of Relativity. But that wasn't his greatest discovery. What was bigger than that was his discovery of *parallel worlds,* 'cept he died before he could prove the physics of it all."

"Parallel worlds?"

"Yeah, you know, like *time travel*," Darrell said. "You don't need a machine or nothing like in H.G. Wells' book *The Time Machine*. That's what Einstein discovered. You see, he felt that human beings measure time the wrong way."

"How's that?"

"Humans measure time in seconds, minutes, hours, days, and so forth," Darrell said. "Einstein measured time differently, and that's how he discovered time travel. He showed me how. That's where I was when that waiter came. I didn't disappear into thin air. I just moved into the future by about five minutes. It's pretty easy to do once you know how to do it. With his little trick, you could travel to the future or the past just as easy as sitting here drinking a beer."

Darrell looked at his watch. Rolex, of course. He pointed to the hands on the watch and said, "This is the time you can understand. See the little hand? See the big hand? It's time we headed back to Portland, wouldn't you say?"

I told the waiter to skip the coffee, and I paid the bill.

We left Bill's Tavern. Who knows what myths the unemployed lumberjacks would create about this giant Japanese guy who downed cheeseburgers as if they were potato chips.

The drive back to Portland was only an hour and a half drive, so a lot of folks make day trips. I was one of those day-trippers. For example, I had gone into the office at my usual time, about nine-thirty in the morning, and realized I just couldn't face the day of boredom and a jerk of a boss. Being in real estate, you have some real flexibility. You know, you're not welded to your desk. You can always be out canvassing for house listings. Or check out some real estate, which could just as conveniently be the type of land found on a golf course or a sandy ocean beach. It's all in the interpretation. So there I was, walking the lonely beach on a Wednesday, talking with a genie.

We had to walk down the beach, back to where I parked my car in a public parking lot.

"I'll drive," Darrell said, extending his hand for the keys to my Toyota Camry. At the time, this didn't seem unreasonable. After all, why not let the genie drive?

With Darrell driving, I've never had a stranger or weirder drive. It would have stunned Rod Serling.

Chapter 4

If you were from New York City or Davenport, Iowa, and took this road back to Portland during the daytime, you'd say this was the most scenic trip you had ever made.

You'd drive past mountains where trees grow up the sides so thickly that you can't see any rocks. You'd fly past tumbling streams that you knew had to be special fishing holes for somebody. Along the way, there were a couple of places that you could get coffee and food. Sometimes, I'd stop at one of these places to delay my return to Portland, and all it didn't mean to me. I'd read the morning paper that I had stashed in my briefcase and drink enough coffee to put a buzz on a dead man.

At night, the scenic drive was pretty much defused. It was like driving down a tunnel of darkness. The mountains and the great fishing holes were hidden somewhere in the blackness. The only thing you saw was the centerline of the road and occasionally some oncoming headlights. With Darrell at the wheel, I let my mind shift into neutral. You know, that state where you're not thinking of anything and you're not noticing anything, but you're still alive. I was jolted out of this mind mushiness when Darrell pulled off the road.

"I gotta have some dessert and coffee," Darrell said. He parked the Toyota in front of a diner.

At one time or another, I'd stopped at each of the handful of restaurants scattered along the way back to Portland. I had never seen this diner before. Darrell must have made a wrong turn someplace.

"Where are we?" I asked.

"On the way back to Portland," Darrell said. He walked into the diner with me following.

The place was packed with travelers. Let me tell you, when you stop at one of these restaurants at night on your way back to Portland, you are lucky to see two or three people—that includes the waitress. In this diner, folks occupied every table and booth. Only two empty stools were open at the counter. We took those two places.

A beefy counterman came over to us. He was wearing a starched white t-shirt, khakis, and a white paper hat. The hat and t-shirt had a printed signature on them that looked like *Mack's*.

Mack looked a lot like the cook Mel on that old TV show Alice.

"Darrell! Long time no see!" the beefy guy said, extending his hand.

Darrell shook it. He introduced me, and I shook the guy's hand too.

"Been traveling, Mack," Darrell said. *Traveling*, I thought, that's what you call going seven thousand miles in a can of spray paint?

"Well, I've got just the dessert for you," Mack said. "It's something I've been working on, keeping me up nights. Also, I'm coming closer to perfecting my coffee."

"Mack's always trying to improve the best," Darrell told me. "He's got the best pie, but he's gonna make it better. He's got the best coffee, but he's gonna make that better too."

"That's right. Even Starbucks thinks mine is better. They've been trying to buy the formula for the past six months."

"So, business still looks great," Darrell said, looking around the diner.

"All the time, it's busy. It *is* great!" Mack said with a big smile.

"Long hours?" Darrell asked.

"You bet, but it's funny, I have more energy each day than the previous day. It's like my work *feeds me energy*—ever since you taught me about *ewe*." Mack said. "Pie and coffee for you both?" Darrell nodded, and Mack hustled off to the kitchen.

"He's...he's...one of your 'Wish' guys?" I asked Darrell.

Darrell nodded, yes.

"What's this about you teaching him *you*? That doesn't make much sense to me."

"Ewe," Darrell corrected me. Then he spelled it out, "E-W-E"

"Ewe?" I asked.

"Ewe."

"Like a female sheep?"

"Nope. And it's not the language of the people that inhabit Ghana."

"What's that?"

"Ewe. That's what their language is called," Darrell said, then he spelled it again, "E-W-E Ewe. I know their language too. Wanna hear?"

I shook my head no. "Let's go back to what Mack said, 'You taught me about ewe.' What's E-W-E?"

Mack set down cups of steaming coffee in front of Darrell and me. The aroma reached up and grabbed my nostrils. "Wow," I said, "that's good enough just to smell." Mack smiled. I took a sip. It tasted even better than it smelled.

"How could coffee be *this* good?" I asked.

"*Esia ye nye coffee nyuiutor le xexame*," Darrell said.

"Pardon?" I said.

"That was Ewe for 'it's the best coffee in the world.'"

"So, Darrell, tell me about this E-W-E," I said.

Darrell sipped his coffee. "Let's talk about work ethic."

"Work ethic? What's that got to do with E-W-E?"

"The W in E-W-E stands for *Work*. The second E stands for *Ethic*. *W*ork *E*thic," Darrell said.

Mack brought over two pieces of a lemon meringue pie. "You know how Key West is famous for its Key Lime pie?" Mack asked. "Well, that stuff tastes like vanilla compared to my lemon meringue pie. Taste it. I get special lemons from Israel. And I get them fast—right after they're picked; they're flown in."

Wow! It's gotta be the lemons.

Darrell and I both pushed a fork into our piece of pie. Wow! If you ever wanted lemon in a pie, this was it. It sucked in your cheeks until they touched each other inside your mouth. I tempered the taste with some of that terrific coffee.

"I used to think *work ethic* was everything," Darrell said. "You know, the harder you work, the better you'll do. I even thought that work ethic was a *random determinism*."

"Random determinism?" I asked.

"Sure, an accident," Darrell said, "just like there are some people who are born to throw a baseball one hundred miles an hour. You, me, Mack, all these people in this restaurant can't throw a baseball like that. You have to be born with the right muscle structure, bones, everything. You have to be *born* to it; it's not something you can develop. And, the best that I can tell, it's mostly *random*."

I ate another piece of the pie. Wow again!

"If it was handed down from generation to generation, how come the *sons* of all the great pitchers throughout baseball history can't throw the great fastball? Where's Nolan Ryan's son? I don't know, but he's not pitching in the Major Leagues."

I thought about that. I thought about great pro basketball players. Michael Jordan. Larry Bird. Magic Johnson. Their fathers weren't former pro players. Heck, Jordan, Bird, and Magic came from small towns, not from the large cities where the most incredible basketball was supposed to be played. *Random determinism.*

"I thought the same thing with work ethic," Darrell said, taking a huge piece of pie on his fork. "It was like being born with a great pitching arm. If you didn't have a great arm, you couldn't develop one. Sure, you might have been pretty good in Little League or even the low minors, but to make it big-time, you had to be born with a great arm. Same with work ethic. If you didn't have a great work ethic, you couldn't develop one. Sure, you could develop a *decent* work ethic, but you had to be *born* with a *great* work ethic. Random determinism."

"So, who wants a great work ethic?" I asked. "I'd rather have a great arm. That would be even better than having a genie grant you one wish."

Darrell looked at me out of the corner of his eye. "You making fun again? I can take that one wish away, you know, pal. Then you got nothing."

"Hey, Darrell, sense of humor, *sense of humor*. Americans have that, you know. Relax. Pal."

He looked at me, trying to determine if I was making fun of him.

He shook off any imagined slight and said, "Now, I've seen some great work ethic around the world. My own countrymen have a great work ethic. Twelve-hour days, devotion to the company. Japan is a *country* of great work ethic. A lot of it is forced, but they put on a pretty good show of work. Sort of like the guy who doesn't have a great arm, but he battles his way through the minor leagues to finally reach his pinnacle, Triple-A."

"Mack was like that," Darrell said, pointing his fork at the big beefy guy now waiting on somebody at the end of the counter. "Worked hard. Lotta, lotta hours. What'd it get him?"

"Looks like a pretty good business," I said.

"Nah," Darrell said, "I'm not talking about now. I'm talking about then. Mack worked hard, really hard. All it got him was a little bit older and deeper in debt. Nah, a great work ethic is overrated. I've seen people with random determinism that gave them great—really great—work ethics, but it wasn't enough. Sure, they might have been a little more successful than if they hadn't had that incredible work ethic, but not enough for it to count."

Before I could ask Darrell to explain what the first "E" in E-W-E was, he got up and straightened out his suit. "Let me show you something," he said.

I hadn't quite finished my lemon meringue pie. "C'mon," he said, walking between the tables toward the wall across the room that was a floor-to-ceiling mirror, making the room seem even larger.

Where was he going? I thought. There wasn't an exit at that end of the diner, nor were the restrooms located at that end. He must be going to see somebody. I turned back to my lemon meringue pie, scooped up the last piece, and turned just in time to see Darrell walk through the mirror. That's right, *he walked through the mirror and disappeared.*

I looked around the room. Nobody had seemed to notice. They were busy eating, drinking coffee, talking, and laughing.

I walked to the mirror. About a foot away from it, I stopped and just stared at the glass, seeing if I could see through it. I couldn't. I just saw myself staring into the mirror. I reached out and touched the mirror. My hand didn't go through. All I felt was the mirror.

Darrell's arm reached out of the mirror, grabbed me by the wrist, and yanked me through. I'll assume you've never been yanked through a mirror, so you might be wondering about the experience. It was underwhelming. It was just like being yanked from one room to the next.

The room I was yanked to was precisely the same as the room that I had been yanked from. Except it was different. Instead of a diner filled with hungry, laughing people, only a haggard-looking couple was sitting at the counter.

Darrell pulled me over to a booth.

"Remember what I told you about Einstein?" Darrell asked me.

I nodded, "Parallel worlds."

"Right. Maybe there is hope for you, pal. We're now in a parallel world to the one we just left."

Mack came over from behind the counter. He looked the same, but there was something different. It's not that he had shaved his beefy hairy arms or anything. He just didn't *seem* to be the same. He seemed tired, worn down.

"What can I get you?" he asked. I looked at Darrell. Mack hadn't recognized Darrell. Darrell's the type of guy that if you met him, you'd remember him. *Parallel worlds*. I was starting to get it.

Darrell said, "Coffee and a piece of pie."

I said, "Just coffee for me."

Mack walked back to the counter.

"He didn't recognize you," I said to Darrell. "What parallel world are we in, anyway?"

"Two years ago," Darrell said. "See any difference in Mack?"

"Yeah. Over there," I said, pointing to the other world beyond the mirror, "he seemed to have so much *passion*, so much *joy* running the diner. Over here, he seems like he's got the flu or something. You know, like he would like to just leave and go to bed."

"That's not all that's different," Darrell said. "Wait till you taste the coffee and see the pie."

As if on cue, Mack brought the coffee and a wedge of a brownish thing on a plate. He laid down the check and went back to the counter.

"You're probably wondering what that is," Darrell said, pointing to the thing on the plate. "Apple. Apple pie."

It looked like Mack had put a dog turd with whipped cream on a plate and put it on the table as some weird practical joke.

"You're going to eat it?" I asked.

"Nope," Darrell said. "God knows I could down a whole pie, maybe two or three, but I'll pass on this one." Darrell pushed the piece of pie to the far corner of the booth, beyond our field of vision.

"Mack puts in more hours now than he does on the other side of that mirror," Darrell said. "Not that he takes much time off over there, but here he practically lives at this joint. The great work ethic is wasted. That's not ewe."

That led me to ask what the first "e" was in E-W-E.

"*Effective,*" Darrell said, "as in *Effective* Work Ethic. E-W-E is *not* just a mountain of hours. If you're just putting in the long hours and not being terrifically effective for all that time spent, you're just like an *observer* watching your career go nowhere. And then one day your career ends, and you, the observer, says 'That's it?' That's all, folks. Then you'd just observe yourself doing nuthin' in retirement—going out to the mailbox to fetch your mail would be your big event of the day. Then you die. I can show you better than tell you. Mack is 'Exhibit A' regarding E-W-E. You're probably wondering what happened to Mack? How come he changed?" Darrell said.

I nodded.

"A can of whipped cream," he said.

"Huh?"

"One day, somebody ordered a piece of apple pie—he must've been a stranger—and Mack shook up a new can of whipped cream. He shook it and shook it, pressed the nozzle, and *voila!* Yours truly popped out into his awful kitchen."

"Whipped cream can?"

"The vessel ain't important," Darrell said. "After all, you can't find too many Aladdin lamps like the old days. You gotta take what you can get to circulate."

I wanted to ask him how he jumped from vessel to vessel, but he jumped up from the booth and said, "Let's go; you've seen enough here. I got something else to show you."

He threw a five-dollar bill on the table and walked like a man on a mission to where else, but back through the mirror. This mirror, however, was on a different wall. I quickly got up from the booth, took one glance at the apple pie in the corner of the table, winced a little bit, and casually, as if I had been doing it for my entire life, walked right to the mirror. I stopped. Darrell reached through the mirror and pulled me through.

When I was halfway in the diner that I was leaving and halfway in the place I was stepping into, I heard, *"Hey, Darrell! Good to see you, friend."*

It was Mack. By now, Mack was probably used to Darrell walking through mirrors.

The diner was about half full. I followed Darrell to two open stools at the counter.

By the time I got to the stool, Mack had already delivered two cups of coffee.

"Who's your friend?" Mack asked.

Darrell introduced me again, and we shook hands again.

"Try the coffee," Mack said. I would like to have said that he was beaming, but that sounds a little too corny. But he *was* beaming, almost as if he was showing off a grandchild.

"That's very good, Mack," Darrell said after he took a sip. "Very, very good. How did you do it? Your other stuff was quite lousy, you know."

"Well, it wasn't easy, but it was easy, d'you know what I mean?"

I didn't know what he meant.

"What did you do first?" Darrell asked.

"Well, after you….ah…left…after we first met, I stayed late in the kitchen after it closed. I just sat there," he said. "I just sat there looking. I didn't like what I saw. You know, over the years, this kitchen got pretty greasy and grimy. The next day I rented one of those steam cleaners, and that night I worked all night long cleaning the place. Once I got started, I asked myself, 'What's it gonna take to make this kitchen look like it was brand new?' That became my benchmark. Heck, I did *everything* to make the kitchen look brand new, including painting the place. Just getting rid of all that grease and grime made my coffee a little bit better."

I glanced over at the service window that opened to the kitchen. From what I saw inside the kitchen, it *still* looked brand new.

I took another sip of coffee. It wasn't quite as good as the coffee that Darrell and I had in the 'first' diner. And, the aroma didn't navigate as well up into your nostrils. But it was a darned good cup of coffee.

"The second thing I did was figure out how I could get coffee direct from Java, Indonesia," Mack said.

"Why Indonesia?" I asked.

"That's the best coffee in the world," Mack said. "But you just can't get it from your normal suppliers. I found a supplier that had some, then I bought some Kona coffee, and then I bought some amazing Brazilian stuff."

He then turned to Darrell and said, "I've been working with different blends since you left. I'm getting close, I think, to the best cup of coffee in the world."

Darrell nodded. "Close."

"But it'll get better," Mack said. "I worked out a way to get *fresh* coffee beans—I mean *really* fresh. Through the Internet, I found a coffee grower in Java, Indonesia that will FedEx coffee beans to me the *day* they are ready. I get my first shipment tomorrow. I can hardly wait to try it—I feel like a kid waiting for Christmas."

"That must be expensive," I said.

"Sure it is," Mack said. "But these 'coffee bars' are charging three to five bucks and even more for a cup of coffee. I can charge a lot less than that, make a decent profit, and you'll be getting the best cup of coffee in the world."

Mack saw a customer motion for more coffee. "Excuse me for a minute," Mack said, grabbing the coffee pot and scooting over to the customer.

"What time is it?" I asked Darrell.

Darrell looked at his Rolex. "Nine thirty-seven," he said.

"No, I don't mean clock time. I mean *when is this*…you know in Einstein's parallel worlds, which world are we in?"

"*Ah-so*," Darrell said. "About two months after that," Darrell said, motioning back toward the mirror that we had just walked through. "And about two years before…before the 'first diner.'"

I nodded. If anyone had overheard us, there was no way they would understand what we were talking about. I wasn't sure of this whole thing myself, but I was trying to roll with the punches the best I could.

Mack was back. "I'm working on a lemon meringue pie," Mack said. "It's not ready yet for you to try, but I'm getting closer. I want to make my lemon meringue pie more famous than Key Lime pie. It's all in the lemons, you know. I'm experimenting with a different lemon from Israel. Flown directly to me."

Mack saw another customer, and he was off like a greyhound.

"See the difference?" Darrell asked me. "The one constant thing in the three Mack's Diners that we visited via parallel worlds was *work ethic*. Mack worked hard in all three. He's no slouch. But in the 'present' diner, and this one, he's been using E-W-E. *Effective* Work Ethic. Can you see the difference?"

"Sure. It's like walking into a dark room and turning on a light. Why? It can't be just coffee and lemon meringue pie."

Darrell laughed. "You'll see."

"Let's go," Darrell said. "See ya, Mack," he yelled, dropping a few dollars on the counter. He pivoted and walked toward the door with me following.

"Hey, don't we have to go through the mirror again?" I asked.

"New trick," he said, "Pay attention." We stepped through the open doorway into the night. There was my car. We got in and drove off into the night, leaving this mysterious diner. As before, Darrell drove.

"I don't know what his wish was," I said, "Or his *two* wishes—you probably didn't penalize him one wish—but he sure is a lively guy. It's strange, I don't equate *joy* with people working in a diner, but he sure has it."

"That he does, that he does," Darrell said.

After a few minutes of silence and mulling over what I had just seen, I said, "I bet I do know what his two wishes were."

"You think so, eh? What d'ya want to lose?" Darrell asked. "Would you want to go *double or nothing* on your one wish?"

I had already lost half of my wishes, so I thought I better not risk the last one. A wish in hand is better than two in the bush, I guess, so I declined.

Darrell laughed. "You would have lost."

"Coffee and lemon meringue pie," I said. "Mack wanted to have the best coffee and lemon meringue pie in the world."

"Wrong on both counts," Darrell said. "Mack *will* have the best coffee and *will* have the best lemon meringue pie, but those weren't his wishes. Not even close."

When we arrived on the outskirts of Portland, Darrell pulled to the side of the road. "See that Denny's across the street," he said, pointing. I nodded. "Pick me up there at ten tomorrow morning."

He jumped out of the car. The last words I heard from him that night were *Grand Slam Breakfasts*. That's plural. Each Grand Slam Breakfast has, I think, three eggs, three pancakes, three pieces of bacon, and three sausages. If Darrell mirrored his breakfast eating to his cheeseburger extravaganza, he would knock down twelve eggs, twelve pancakes, twelve pieces of bacon, and twelve sausages tomorrow morning. And maybe a partridge in a pear tree.

He was out of sight by the time I slid over behind the steering wheel. Where he was going to sleep that night, God only knows. It wasn't going to be in that aerosol paint can. The can was still lying on the floor in the back of my car. That would probably be a safer place for me to sleep. My wife sure wasn't going to believe this.

Chapter 5

The next morning, there he was, standing in front of Denny's, dressed like a power broker waiting for his limo. He wore a different Italian suit. It must be great to be a genie and carry your wardrobe in a wish.

Darrell had probably already knocked down three or four Grand Slam Breakfasts, but he didn't look any bigger.

Before I could pull a U-turn, he jumped into an opening in the traffic, looking like a running back weaving around a slew of tacklers. Quick, he was, and agile. Within a flash, he was climbing into the passenger seat of my car. Wow, he could move fast for a big guy—a big guy who had probably put on an eating exhibition that the waitresses would be talking about for weeks to come.

"Let's go," Darrell said.

"Where to?" I asked.

"Airport," Darrell said.

As we approached the airport, Darrell told me to pull off into a road with a grouping of warehouses.

"Detour," he said. "We're going to go back in time first, then we gotta make a couple of stops, and then we'll go to the golf course."

"Golf?" I asked.

"Don't worry about it," Darrell said, pulling into a parking spot in front of a small warehouse. He was out of the car like a jackrabbit.

"C'mon," he said, waving his hand like I was in a race or something.

We stepped into the warehouse, and after a few steps, I felt a little lightheaded. It seemed like I was stepping into an optical illusion because as I walked, I realized I was, astonishingly, in the *airport,* the Portland International Airport. It was crazy-bustling like it had been *before* the pandemic.

I looked back through the windows from where we entered, and it wasn't the lot where I had just parked my car. It was the airport! It was a mess of cars sliding in and out of spots to drop off passengers.

I looked at Darrell, trying to get some understanding of this strange illusion he'd just pulled off.

"Don't ask," Darrell said. "Let's go."

We hurried along with some of those harried travelers trying to catch their flights. It seemed everybody was on a hopped-up treadmill inside the terminal, except for the crowd waiting in the lines to get ticketed. They seemed to be fidgeting up-tempo.

"C'mon over here," Darrell said, motioning to me. "I want you to see this."

I walked over to where Darrell was standing. It was between the ropes that separated the coach passengers from those in first class. It seemed like there were a thousand people in the coach line and two or three in the first-class line.

"Watch this," Darrell said, nodding toward the ticket agents.

Several of the agents looked frazzled. I guess anybody in that position would be. One agent wasn't. It looked like *he* was having fun. He even greeted each passenger with a smile and a hello.

This agent was an African-American man in his 40s. His demeanor reminded me, strangely, of a character like Frosty the Snowman. This agent didn't have a button nose or two eyes made of coal, of course, but he had the presence of Frosty. You know, cheery. Happy. Jolly.

"That's George," Darrell said, nodding toward Frosty.

George had fingers that could fly.

"He's one of yours?" I asked, thinking right after I asked that it was such a dumb question.

Darrell nodded, smiling.

George's hands were a blur on the computer keyboard. If he chose to, he could have made a fortune as a three-card monte dealer on the sidewalks of New York.

It seemed that once he took a passenger's ticket, his hands had a mind of their own as he was talking, even joking, with the passenger. I saw other agents doing a modern version of the hunt and peck typing system. And they looked deep in concentration like they were trying to solve some 1000-piece puzzle that only they could see. Or perhaps they just didn't want to talk to the passengers. After all, who would want to speak to these hyped-up, sweating, arrogant, angry, nervous passengers? Punch out the ticket and get them out of here! But as fast as they would like to get them out of there and out of their sight, George was really cranking them through more quickly. A lot faster. If he was paid by piecework, he'd be making a fortune.

"Pretty interesting, eh?" Darrell said. I nodded. If I hadn't been watching it all, I wouldn't believe that one agent could handle as many passengers as at least two other agents. It's not as if the other agents were rookies or dullards; they looked experienced; they sure looked like they were working hard. It's just that George practically whisked the customers through like magic.

"Well, watch this," Darrell said. "This next customer will really challenge George. This will slow him down." He nodded toward an ancient Japanese man who inched, step by little quavering step, to the counter in front of Frosty. "I don't think this fella knows English too well."

When the little Asian had finally reached the counter, George bowed slightly.

I could hear George's greeting. It sounded like "Ohio go zai mas."

"Good morning," Darrell translated.

The Japanese man said something I couldn't hear clearly, but I knew it wasn't in English.

Before the Japanese man could hand his ticket over the counter, George whipped out a business card from his shirt pocket. With two hands, George held the card out to the old man. As he extended his arms so that the old man could take the card, George bowed again, his eyes diverted downwards.

"One side of the card is printed in English," Darrell said, "the other side in Japanese. He's handing that old man the Japanese side up. Respect."

The old man took the card and bowed also.

It was then business as usual for George. George took the man's ticket, and within a microsecond his fingers raced over the keyboard. In one fluid motion, George slapped a destination sticker on the handle of the old man's suitcase that had been placed in the slot between agents. George whisked the suitcase onto the conveyor belt in the same motion, turning back to pull out the man's boarding pass from the printer. It was almost as if George was a sleight-of-hand magician who made a suitcase disappear, and a boarding pass appear. All the while, George was speaking to the man in Japanese. A three-card monte dealer would be stunned at the quickness.

George then squeezed through the slot where the old man's suitcase had been and gently took the man by the elbow and helped him navigate through the crowd. Once he was in the clear, George bowed deeply; the old man bowed and went tottering off. George stood there, watching him disappear into the crowd. Only then did he head back to the counter.

I looked back at the counter. The same passengers who had been working with the other agents were still there. Some sagged against the counter, waiting. Others impatiently tapped their feet as if that could pump up the process. While these passengers were waiting, fidgeting, sweating, George had processed his elderly non-English speaking passenger, who could have been a real logjam. He had processed this old gentleman faster than the other agents had processed theirs. Amazing.

If Darrell hadn't had me stand there and watch this whole thing like it was a baseball game, I'm sure I wouldn't have noticed George from the other agents. His movements weren't hurried, they weren't herky-jerky, he wasn't perspiring, he wasn't out of breath. It looked like he was just casually taking his time. And yet, he was processing passengers about twice as quickly as any other agent. Amazingly, it looked like he was enjoying himself!

"When did...ah...you and George...meet?" I asked.

Darrell laughed. "About five years ago, but what you're really interested in was *how* did we meet. Right?"

"Well, sure," I said. "With me, you come out of a can of spray paint on the beach. With Mack, it was a can of whipped cream."

"With George, I was in a can of STP," Darrell said.

"Can of STP?"

"Yep, a good old can of STP," Darrell said. "Slippery stuff, you know. Really, *really* slippery. George was just about to add it to his crankcase to try to save his old Plymouth from getting a three-hundred-dollar valve job. He popped the top of the STP and *voila! Here's Johnny.*"

We watched for a couple of minutes more. Darrell looked at his Rolex and said, "George will be on break in about fifteen minutes. I'd like to introduce you to him."

"I'd like that," I said.

"In the meantime, follow me. I want to show you something," Darrell said, pivoting away from our vantage point like he was on skates. Man, this guy was nimble for a big guy.

As usual, I had to take a lot of quick steps to catch up to Darrell. Like a bowling ball barreling down a lane, he was heading straight for a gray metal door that had *Maintenance* stenciled on it. Darrell reached into his pocket and pulled out a large ring with about twenty keys on it.

He thumbed through them, finding the one he wanted, and inserted it into the lock. He opened the door and politely ushered me inside.

It was a small room filled with stuff you would think would be there, like mops, buckets, an old-fashioned carpet sweeper. We could barely stand in the room without bumping into each other. Facing the door that we entered was another door. Darrell thumbed through the keys again and inserted one into the lock of the second door.

He opened it and again politely ushered me through. I stepped over a bucket and into the terminal. Oh-oh, here we go, *time traveling* again. What I saw was the same Portland airport terminal, but it was different, a lot different. It was smaller, the carpeting worn thin in places, there weren't nearly as many travelers, and there was no construction going on at all.

"Years ago," Darrell said, anticipating the question mark on my face. "Nice little airport," he said, and he was off again like a dog after a bone with me scrambling after him.

We ended up at the vantage point where we had been observing George just moments before. The tableau looked about the same, except there were fewer travelers and fewer ticket agents. But you know something, *everybody* looked the same as in the previous terminal except for George. Now he looked just as harried as the other agents. They looked as annoyed as the travelers.

I watched George work. He didn't greet people. He just waited for them to hand him their ticket.

When George got the ticket in his hand, he looked at the computer as if it should be doing something independently. George's fingers pecked at the keyboard. He put his hand up to his chin while he stared at the computer screen. He tapped something else on the keyboard. He stared again. The passenger looked at his watch about every twenty seconds. My, how time doesn't fly. Eventually, the passenger was on his way, pushing himself into a spastic airport trot.

"Well, what d'ya think?" Darrell asked.

"His boss must have jumped all over him at some point," I said.

"Oh, really," Darrell said. "Why do you say that?"

"You can just tell. Here, he's moving in slow motion. Over there," I said, pointing to the maintenance door, "he's hustling; he's working twice as hard as anybody."

"So, it was his boss?"

"Yep, probably."

"You know, you're missing something," Darrell said. "What's the one thing—just *one* thing that the newer version of Mack and George have in common?"

I stood there, thinking for a minute. Darrell said something that I didn't quite catch. "What?" I asked.

"It's something that you said about Mack. Do you remember?"

I didn't.

"*Joy?*" he said.

"I did say that, didn't I?" I said. "Yes, Mack and George certainly seemed to be enjoying themselves. Working hard, but enjoying themselves anyway."

"You also mentioned *passion,*" Darrell said.

"Yeah, Mack really did have a passion for what he was doing. Everybody could tell. George had that passion too."

"Take a look at George now," Darrell said. George was laboring through the processing of a ticket. "As you suggested, could a boss bring *joy* and *passion* by getting all over him? He might be able to make him work a little harder for a short time while standing next to him with a gun pointed at his head, but could he instill *joy* and *passion*?"

"No, no, of course not," I said. "You're right. It wasn't the boss." I was thinking of my boss. At one time, he had pushed me all over the place, trying to motivate me, and all I did was figure out a better way of faking it. Heck, if they gave out Academy Awards for faking it on a real job and not just in the movies, I'd have a bunch of those little statuettes on my mantle right now. Now my boss didn't push me so much; he just accepted my mediocrity.

Darrell looked at his watch. "Well, time to meet George," he said.

This time I anticipated his quick departure and was walking in lockstep with him to the maintenance door. You know, you don't have to be an Einstein to pick up this time travel stuff.

We walked through the maintenance closet and entered the newer, bustling terminal. We wove through the travelers to the food court. As we walked, a few dark clouds started to slide into my mind. I thought, *what's wrong with this picture?* Not the picture of these weird time-warp journeys, but the picture of *George*. I could understand the transformation of Mack. After all, he was on a quest to develop the best cup of coffee and the best lemon meringue pie. Heck, if he even came close to achieving that, he could make a fortune. McDonald's Big Mac ain't even close to being perfect, but it paid billions to Ray Kroc.

But George? He could handle *at least twice as many passengers* as any other ticket agent in the world, and he'd still be getting the same pay as the worst ticket agent bumbling through the day. The signs here appeared to be pointing toward some crazy *cult*. You know, those people who drank the poisoned Kool-Aid believing that they were doing a beautiful thing. I wondered, was this some loony genie creating a cult of some sort?

George was sitting on a stool at a round table with a Wendy's double burger, fries, and Coke.

Darrell introduced me to George.

"Lunch," George said, pointing to his hamburger. "I start here at five-thirty in the morning."

We made some small talk about the Portland Trail Blazers, then Darrell must have sensed my mood change and decided to flame up the conversation.

"My friend here," Darrell said to George, "thinks you work too hard."

George laughed, putting down his hamburger. "I put in my eight-hour day," he said, "just like everybody else."

That was all I needed to let some of those doubting demons in my mind voice their opinions. I said, "But you're processing at least twice as many passengers as anybody else. We were watching."

"I don't count how many people I process," George said, stuffing a french fry in his mouth. "That's almost irrelevant."

"That's not *relevant*?" I said, feeling my always-reliable negative juices bubbling. Those negative juices seemed to always be simmering below the surface, but I would rarely let them out in the form of words. I'd instead just mumble to myself how stupid my boss was or how many rear ends a neighbor must have kissed to get the promotion. But today, in this goofy time-warp world, no Kool-Aid for me. "You're doing twice the work of anybody else, and you're getting paid, I assume, the same? Somebody might consider that you're being taken advantage of. So, George, to you, what *is* relevant?"

"Well, if you can ask a question like that," George said, "you're probably not going to like my answer, or you probably won't understand it." George then turned his head to Darrell as if he wanted to say *Who is this idiot, anyway?*

"Explain it to me, anyway, if you can," I said.

Darrell left the table, saying he was going to get us something to eat. I guess four Grand Slam breakfasts weren't enough.

"By your questions, it seems to lead to pay, to money," George said. "Well, money *is* important. Money *is* relevant. I know how much money I'm going to make. Sure, I won't make more for processing more travelers. But *I know what I'm going to make* for a forty-hour week. To me, that is important. Can I make more if I do something else for a living? Maybe. There's a lot of guys that I punch tickets for that make a lot of money. But they're on a fast track; they take a lot of risks. I don't want the risks. I don't want the fast track. I don't want the politics that it might take. So, I look to one thing."

"One thing?" I asked. This started to sound like *one wish*. Darrell returned with two single-patty hamburgers from Wendy's, two fries, and two Diet Cokes. He pushed one of each toward me. Looking at what he was going to eat, he must figure that he was on a starvation diet.

"As I was saying," George said, "the one thing I look for is to have fun."

I looked over at Darrell. He knew what I was thinking—the one wish for George was to have fun. He answered my thoughts with a slight head shake from side to side as if to say, *Nope*.

"How can you have *fun* processing tickets?" I asked.

"Well, I can see this isn't for you," George said, "and that's fine, it's right for *me*. It isn't just the punching of the tickets—that's just something mechanical. I like to look at the bigger picture."

"The bigger picture?"

"Sure. Traveling isn't a joyride these days—crowded airports, long lines, crowded planes, late planes, small seats, one teeny package of pretzels. If you do much of it, traveling isn't fun. So, I try to make at least one small memory that *something* on the passenger's trip was pleasant. That something is me."

Very honorable, I felt like saying with striking sarcasm, but if this guy was that stupid to believe he could make a difference, I wasn't going to change him. I thought I'd challenge this idiocy in a different, less sledgehammer approach. I said, "How can you make it a little more pleasant?"

"Do you fly much?" George asked.

"A little," I said.

"One of the things that must bug you while flying is waiting in lines."

Only a genius could have said that, my demons said to me, but I just nodded.

"If you were traveling, waiting in line, and you came to me, there are two things I could do for you: be nice, and process your ticket as fast as possible."

I nodded again, holding back my sarcasm at such an obvious statement.

"The only way you notice is if I work too slow," George said, "then it aggravates you. If I'm fast, you don't say, 'W*ow, what speed you have.*' But by working fast, I'm not rubbing salt into a wound. To get fast, I mean really fast, I had to work on it. Most of us agents were decent typists. I, however, wanted to speed up the process personally. The best way was to take typing lessons. *Speed* typing lessons. Sure, I took typing in high school. Fifty words a minute on a manual typewriter. That was pretty good. Now I type over ninety words a minute. But speed wasn't enough. I needed more."

"A smile?" I asked, still doing a good job of holding down my sarcasm.

"Yes, that is important, but it's not in reference to speed. I wanted more speed than my typing could give me. I forced myself to learn the macros of the airline's computer ticketing system."

George explained that macros were keyboard shortcuts in the computer program that the airline used. In some cases, instead of typing 12 keystrokes to process a ticket, he could use a macro and use just three keystrokes to get the same results. Most of the agents used just some of the macros; George used them all.

"One day, a technician was out here to tweak our computer," George said, "and he and I took a break together. I asked him about the macros. He told me that I could create some of my own macros to speed things along, and he showed me how. When I use typing shortcuts, I can actually input faster than I can physically type. Now that is real speed."

"But what does it get you?" I asked. "It's not more pay. A promotion?"

"No, I don't get more pay," George said. "And, I'm not looking for a promotion. Promotions have been offered to me several times, but I'm in my forties and I'm having fun at what I'm doing. I'm putting in the same amount of hours as a few years ago when I wasn't having any fun at all. If I'm going to spend about two-thirds of my waking hours at work—including driving to and from work—and I do have to work, I might as well have fun. I've read stuff that says you should get a job doing something that interests you. With me, that's golf. Well, I think that's a crock. I enjoy golf when I'm not working. And, I get to play for free because I'm a part-time volunteer starter one day a week at a local course, which provides me free rounds. Because I'm a ticket agent, I get special travel deals, and I play golf all over the country. I enjoy being a ticket agent; I have predictable hours; I get off early, giving me the afternoons for golf. It's a good job, pays decent, and it's a lot of fun for me."

"Well, you probably got the other agents miffed at you because it looks like you're showing them up," I said.

"They never really noticed when my typing started to improve," George said, "but once they did, they did sorta think I was showing them up. But then they just got used to it. I've got some good friends here."

I had to admit to myself that it was pretty impressive that this guy went to such lengths to speed up his personal service.

"I like the Japanese part," Darrell said. "Tell him about it, George."

"There's not much to tell," George said. "It gets back to speed. We have one flight a day from Portland to Tokyo. There are quite a few Japanese travelers who aren't completely comfortable with English. They're a little hesitant because they don't want to make a mistake with our language. To speed up the process, I learned *their* language."

Learned their language? This was getting too incredible. This guy must be nuts. "Wait a minute," I said, *"you learned Japanese to speed up the process?"*

George nodded, smiling.

"How long did it take?" I asked.

"Not as long as you think," George said. "I started with a course at a junior college. I liked it, so then I took another. Then one of those mail-order courses with tapes. I listened to the tapes forty-five minutes a day while commuting for two years."

"George has made a lot of Japanese friends because of this," Darrell said.

"That's been an unanticipated benefit," George said.

Ah so, I thought, there was some method behind this madness. George has some deal going with the Japanese.

"How so?" I asked.

"Well, I've gotten to know some of the frequent travelers from Japan. When they're waiting in line, they'll let another passenger through until I'm available. I consider that an honor. As you know, working for an airline, we get to travel basically for free. When I let some of these frequent Japanese travelers know that my wife and I were planning on visiting Japan, they couldn't have been nicer. We've visited Japan three times now, and on each trip, one of my frequent travelers from Japan hosted my wife and me. They wouldn't let us buy anything. They showered us with some nice gifts. And, we played golf. Each trip has been a little more marvelous than the previous trip."

George took the last bite of his Wendy's. "I gotta get back to work. Nice meeting you, Elmer," he said to me. Then he said with a wink, "I hope you wish for the right thing. I did, and I've never been a happier man."

After George left, Darrell said, "That's a pretty good example of E-W-E. You see, to have a great E-W-E, you don't have to put in longer hours. Heck, George just puts in his eight hours a day just like anybody else there. But he has a highly *Effective Work Ethic*."

Darrell slurped the rest of his Coke and then asked me, "Do you consider George successful?"

"Successful?"

"Yes, successful."

"Well, I guess it all depends on what you use as the benchmarks for measuring success. If it's money, no, George is not particularly successful."

"Is money the only benchmark?" Darrell asked.

"It's an important one," I said.

"If it is, then what about a great social worker? Or a great anthropologist? What about a great third-grade teacher? Using money as the benchmark, they would be considered *un*successful; they could even be considered financial *failures*. I think money probably isn't that important to them. Using money as the measuring stick, Mack and George would certainly be unsuccessful, but look at them—could you say they were unsuccessful? Do you think they *feel* unsuccessful?"

I had seen Mack and George at work. They had the joy of achieving, the passion for work, even if it was a bit weird. I had never known a *joy* or a *passion* connected to work. And, if the benchmark for success did include money, then I've never experienced that either.

But they did indeed have *joy,* and they did indeed have *passion.* How much money would I pay *joy* and *passion* on a job? Such an absurd idea—I don't even know the price tag.

Chapter 6

Darrell told me to drive to a large office building downtown.

I didn't question the destination. After all, if you buy into the genie thing at all, then you buy in all the way. When I woke up this morning, I had a distinct feeling this genie stuff—meaning Darrell—was downright real, crazy as it all seemed to be. So, here I am driving a genie to downtown Portland, Oregon.

We parked in the basement of the large office building, took the elevator to the ground floor. We stepped into an office across from the elevators. It was a brokerage house. There was a large LED that only featured stock symbols and prices scrolling across the screen. To me, those stock symbols were as meaningful as if they were in Sanskrit. Darrell, however, stood there watching it, nodding, smiling.

"You can read that?" I asked Darrell.

Darrell could read Sanskrit and stock symbols.

"Yep," he said, "that's another language, stock symbols. I didn't even count that in the 118 languages I know. But this one makes the most money."

"You play the market?" I asked.

"Sure," Darrell said, "I make a fortune every day, even when the market is down."

If there ever was a sure thing in this world, I thought, Darrell had it. Take a little trip into the future, look at *The Wall Street Journal*, come back, and make a fortune. Me? I didn't have those supernatural skills, of course, so I didn't play the stock market.

"Can you give me a couple of tips?" I asked.

"I am," Darrell said. "That's why I'm here with you."

"No...I mean *stock* tips."

Darrell laughed and said, "Okay."

I waited.

"If you were a stock, would you buy *yourself* right now?" Darrell asked.

I snorted a laugh.

"I'm serious," Darrell said, "no jokes. Let me ask you again: *If you were a stock, would you buy yourself right now?*"

I thought about that for a moment. I'm sorry to say that I probably wouldn't. I'm not sure I'd classify myself as a loser stock, but I sure ain't a high-flyer. Better to put my money in a certificate of deposit than myself.

Darrell didn't wait for me to think anymore. "How about Mack?" Darrell asked. "If he was a stock, would you buy him now?"

"Sure," I answered. "There's a lot of upside with Mack."

"Well, *I* would buy stock in *you*," Darrell said. "Yes, the market in you is depressed, been depressed for a long time. But you've got that one wish. That's big. That is a genuine *game-changer*. If you wish for the correct thing, your stock will skyrocket. Is it worth the risk to buy stock in you? We'll see."

We stood there watching the stock symbols.

"Okay, let's go," Darrell said.

"We're done here?" I asked. "We're not going to meet somebody?"

"We're done," Darrell said. "I just wanted to show you the stock symbols rushing by. Sorta like life, isn't it? Let's go to the Rose Garden."

"The Rose Garden?" I asked. "Where the Portland Trail Blazers play?"

"Yup, let's go."

Chapter 7

I assumed we weren't going to the Rose Garden to see the Blazers play since it was still morning, but I guessed that anything could happen with this time travel stuff. Sure enough, when we arrived at the Rose Garden, there wasn't the heavy traffic for a game. Darrell directed me to the underground parking lot, which I had never been in before. When I went to a Trail Blazer game, I'd usually hunt for a parking spot on the street a few blocks away.

"For executives," Darrell explained.

I nodded. Even though I was a season ticketholder, I had never met a Blazer executive before. I always did my ticket transactions online.

"Park there," he said, pointing to an open spot.

We walked to an elevator with Darrell leading the way like he'd been here before. We took an elevator and stepped into the lobby of the Portland Trail Blazers.

For some reason, I thought it would be fancier. You know, this is Portland's team in the NBA. We play such iconic teams as the Los Angeles Lakers and the New York Knicks. But, the lobby was as plain as if it was an insurance agency.

Darrell checked in with the receptionist. A few moments later, the receptionist said our party was ready for us, and we could go back.

We walked through a wide entrance to see some cubicles and offices. The area seemed quiet, proper, and understated.

A sharply dressed guy in suspenders walked toward us. He must be a big-shot exec—he looked like a *leader,* but then he sat down in a cubicle and put on a headset.

Across the room, Darrell waved to a woman. She was just finishing up a conversation with several men in suspenders. She was attractive, probably in her late thirties, wearing a conservative skirt and blouse and heels. She started to come toward us. It's difficult to describe how she walked. It was like she was gliding—so smooth but quick, confident, vibrant. You could just *feel* her presence from across the room. I assumed she was the administrative assistant to whoever had that corner office. Whoever had that corner office sure had a nice-looking secretary.

"Darrell! How are you doing?" the woman said, hugging him.

Darrell introduced me to her, and we shook hands. I was dying for a cup of coffee, and I was about to ask her if she could get me one when she and Darrell walked into the corner office. She sat behind the big desk.

"Monica is in charge of the business here," Darrell said.

"Can I get you some coffee?" Monica asked, smiling.

I said, "Uh…yes…thank you…black."

Monica got up and walked over to a table that had a thermal pitcher. She poured two cups and delivered them to Darrell and me.

As she sat down, the phone on her desk rang.

"Excuse me," Monica said, "I've been expecting this one call. We're closing on a big sponsorship deal. Stay right there; it'll just be a minute."

I watched her as she was closing this big deal. She was calmly talking as if she were chatting with a friend. If this was a big deal, she sure didn't show it with any stressful emotions. She looked like she was having a terrific time. Even when she pecked some numbers on her computer, she did it with a quiet flair. I was having fun just watching her. That's how you make a big deal in this business, I guess. I heard her say, "OK, it's done. Thank you, Phil. This is a great investment for you."

If you're a salesperson, it's sort of a reflex to look at numbers on somebody's desk. I can even read things upside down. I don't consider this spying. It's more like being professionally nosy. It's a tough habit to break. In this case, I didn't even have to read things upside down; I could see some of the numbers on the computer screen. What jumped out to me was $1,400,000. I'm not sure what constitutes a big deal in the pricey world of NBA basketball, but I'm impressed with a million-four sponsorship. That certainly was a big deal to me. She handled the deal so confidently—it was like she was making a deal for $140 instead of almost halfway to two million dollars.

A salesperson's eyes will also stray to look at things on walls. While she was on the phone, I scanned Monica's walls. There weren't any dead trophy fish hanging on the wall. There were, however, two diplomas. One was a college diploma. The second one showed that Monica had attended a Dale Carnegie course. Now, why would a big-time exec have that diploma up there next to her college diploma?

After she hung up, Monica pushed a button on her phone.

"Monica doesn't have anybody screen her phone calls," Darrell said, referring to the button that she had pushed on the phone.

"That's right," Monica said. "I started in this business in ticket sales with the Philadelphia 76ers of the NBA. Telemarketing, to be exact. I had to make phone calls all day long, trying to talk to executives I had never met about buying a ticket package. I wasted an excessive amount of my time on the so-called phone tag. I vowed that if I ever became a 'big-shot,' I'd eliminate that phone tag. I don't want anybody screening my calls."

Heck, even I, as a real estate salesman, have somebody to answer my phone when I am in the office. I *liked* somebody screening my calls. There were a lot of times I didn't want to talk to certain people. If somebody didn't screen my calls, I'd have to talk to those people when I didn't want to. It was a lot better for an executive assistant to say that I was out of the office and ask if she could take a message. If I ever became a big-shot, I'd want a gatekeeper to protect me from unwanted callers.

"You might have noticed that I pushed the button on my phone to deliver callers to my voicemail," Monica said.

I nodded. I hated voicemail. It was like leaving a message in a black hole.

She pushed a couple of buttons on her phone. Her voicemail message played, "I'm not available right now, but if you leave your name and phone number, I'll get back to you within two hours. If you need immediate assistance, press the pound sign. Thank you for calling."

"*Two hours?*" I asked.

"*Within* two hours," she said, "and I have *never* not returned a call within two hours. Even when I'm traveling, I call in for my voice messages every two hours."

"Do you get many unwanted calls?" Darrell asked.

"Not very many. Occasionally, I get some from people trying to sell something I don't want," Monica said, "but if they're good—really good—on the phone, I have them come in. *They* might be a good candidate for one of our jobs in sales. That's part of what I'm here for —find great people, manage them, and not doing anything to them that would screw them up."

"*Ah-so*," Darrell said, looking around her office. "I'm impressed with the progress you've made in what used to be a male-dominant business."

Monica was impressive. And she got me coffee! She didn't seem to be as severe as some of the women executives I have met. Heck, some of the women I knew in the real estate business were tough hombres. She just seemed like a nice woman...a nice attractive woman.

"I attribute a lot of my success to ewe." Monica said.

Darrell looked at me and spelled it out. "E-W-E, not Y-O-U."

Monica smiled at me as if she were saying, *Yes, I'm one of Darrell's disciples.*

"I first used E-W-E to learn how to become the best ticket salesperson in the telemarketing bullpen with the 76ers," Monica said. "Without E-W-E, I wouldn't have figured it out. Then, when I was promoted to the sales manager position, I found that most of the skills that made me a great ticket salesperson were not the same skills that could make me a great manager. I tried to use those skills when I first became a manager, but most people thought I was a bitch. I *hate* that word, bitch, but they were right. I then used E-W-E to develop the skills I would need to manage. That was key to my promotions—to manage people so they would maximize their abilities. That was more difficult than becoming a great salesperson."

We chatted a little bit more, and then Darrell stood up and said, "Well, Monica, we don't want to take up any more of your time. I just wanted to stop by and say hello. You're doing terrific. I'm really proud of you."

Monica walked us to the lobby of the Blazers office. I lingered a bit as we walked, looking at the Blazer player photos on the wall. They were all heroes of mine. I still had an autograph of Blazer great Clyde Drexler someplace in my office drawer.

Back at my car, driving out of the Rose Garden, I asked Darrell, "So, did Monica *wish* her way to the top? Unlike real estate sales, it doesn't appear that there are very many women in this industry. So, it seems she must have had some extra help—like an extra wish or *two* or even *three*."

Darrell didn't take my bait about the two or three wishes. He said, "You're right, there aren't too many women in this industry, and there are far fewer in the executive suite. She did have one wish, of course, and she used it wisely. And, then she rode the right horse—*herself*. Even with the one wish, it wasn't easy, believe me."

Darrell looked at me, "You a little hungry?" he asked.

"Not really," I said. "Where to next?"

"Back to the airport," he said.

"We're going to visit George again?" I asked.

"You'll see," Darrell said. Then he quickly pointed to the left, tossing his large left arm in front of my vision, providing a blind spot for my driving. "Is that a McDonald's over there? Let's make a quick stop."

Chapter 8

As we approached the airport, Darrell told me to take the same road that led to a grouping of warehouses. We pulled up to the same warehouse but walked to a different door.

Darrell crumpled up the McDonald's wrappers and tossed them into the trash container. Yep, you guessed it—we made a quick pit stop at McDonald's where Darrell had just two Egg McMuffins.

"This is gonna be different," Darrell said.

Different? Like all this time travel stuff was *normal*?

We stepped into the warehouse. It was not the airport. It was a large business office with a sea of cubicles lined up as far as the eye could see. There was a big logo of the Philadelphia 76ers on the far wall.

"We're in Philly?" I whispered to Darrell.

He nodded, smiling. "No jet lag, right?"

I guessed there wasn't jet lag with time travel.

I looked over the room. Men were in the cubicles talking on phones. They weren't a raggedy bunch; they looked successful with ties, long-sleeve white shirts, and, of course, suspenders. There was one thing out of the ordinary that caught my eye. Monica was in one of the cubicles about a third of the way down the large room.

She looked different. Well, I thought, here we go again in parallel worlds.

Monica was not only younger than when I first met her in the Blazers office, but that wasn't the main difference. She was dressed almost like a man. Slacks. Blazer. Even suspenders.

Monica spotted Darrell. She went over to him and shook his hand. Darrell introduced us again.

Monica offered to buy us a cup of coffee. As we walked to an empty lunchroom at the end of the hallway, Darrell whispered to me, "Eleven years ago."

I nodded nonchalantly. I might have even winked. I was getting a real feel for this parallel worlds stuff.

After getting us coffee, Monica said to Darrell, "It's so difficult, Darrell, doing telemarketing sales in the bullpen with all these guys. There are 100 telemarketers here, and I'm the only woman who has stuck around for more than a few days."

"What's so difficult about it?" Darrell asked.

"The men," she said. "This is like a fraternity. I've tried to fit in, but I'm a *woman*, and the only thing a woman is good for in a fraternity is to *party*."

"So, you've decided to *follow the followers*," Darrell said. "I see you've tried to dampen your femininity. That type of thinking will only help you lose your focus."

"I'm just trying to fit in better," Monica said.

Monica had to compete will a floor full of men.

"Won't work," Darrell said. "Yes, by trying to be one of the guys, you might seem to fit in a little better, but your one wish won't come true. I'm not saying you should dress like trash, but be yourself and don't lose your femininity in the process. Go back to the lube jobs, oil changes and tune-ups of your wish, Monica. People respect success, and people respect people who have a *passion* for their job—regardless of gender, race or religion or whatever. When you worry about gender or those other issues—even though they could be real issues—you *lose some of the passion* for the job."

Lube jobs, oil changes, tune-ups? What in the world was Darrell talking about?

"There is one lube job that seems to be working," Monica said.

"Which is?" Darrell asked.

"Well, we are supposed to start making phone calls at 9:00am, not a minute earlier," Monica said. "By that time, all the prospects I call have their assistants in place, ready to shield them from any unwanted telemarketers like me. So, I started making my phone calls at 7:30am from my apartment. I read where many top executives come in that early, but their executive assistants don't. I'm able to make about 40 phone calls before I leave for work at 8:30am."

"Does that work?" Darrell asked.

"Of the 40 phone calls I make, I get usually six or seven connects, meaning I actually talk to the exec, not to some voicemail," Monica said. "Being able to actually talk to the exec, I found I can make an appointment. If I make an appointment with the executive, I'm able to close a sale with that executive about 75% of the time. It might not always be for full-season tickets, but it's a sale for *something*. So, I've been climbing up the sales ladder, and nobody knows why."

Darrell laughed.

"Now I'm expanding the number of appointments I make," Monica said.

"I thought the job was telemarketing," I said. "Do they allow you to go out on sales calls? Wouldn't some salespeople just abuse that?"

"They don't prohibit us from making in-person sales calls," Monica said, "but they don't encourage it. If you do make a personal sales call, you're not reimbursed for your expenses. Parking is expensive here in Philly, so nobody makes sales calls at a prospect's office. Let me tell you, unless it's a guaranteed sale where the prospect says, 'come by my office and pick up the cash,' the sales guys here won't leave the office."

"It takes planning," Monica continued, "but I make about ten sales calls a week where I'm in the prospect's office."

"You're gone from the office that much?" I asked.

"Not really," Monica said. "My first sales call of the day is usually around 8:00am. Our office doesn't open up until 9:00am. Sometimes I can get in two sales calls and waltz into the office around 9:15am or so with a bunch of the other guys."

"I get another three sales calls a week during lunch hour," Monica said.

"You buy them lunch?" I ask. "That must get a little spendy."

"I don't *buy* the prospects lunch," Monica said. "I *visit* them during lunch hour. The same article I read about executives showing up early said that many have lunch in their office at their desk while their executive assistants go out to lunch. If I'm not on a sales call at lunchtime, it's a great time to make more appointment calls at that time. Most of our sales guys here go out to lunch."

"Lastly, many top execs usually work late," Monica said. "So, our day at the office ends at 4:00pm, and they push us all out of here—it's got something to do with the labor laws, and they don't want to end up paying us overtime just to make a few extra phone calls. So, I often have a sales call at 4:30pm—on my own time. If I don't have a sales call, I go to the gym and then start making phone calls at 5:30pm from my apartment. I get the same ratio of connects as in the morning."

"That's a full day," I said.

"I end up working about an hour more than the other salespeople here," Monica said. "That's not much of a price to pay to be more successful. But, it's not like I'm working in a coal mine, and now I find it fun. I even call on Saturday mornings."

"Saturday mornings?" I asked. I worked some weekends at open houses, but I despised it.

"Yep, top execs often go in to work on Saturday mornings," Monica said. "So, I spend about a half-hour every Saturday morning calling the execs I didn't reach during the week. I usually connect to five or six. I've even gone out on appointments on Saturday mornings."

Darrell was nodding like a proud father.

"I admit, Darrell, I got off track a bit on 'being one of the boys,'" Monica said. "But, my new strategies are working wonders. I've been the top salesperson the last two months. And, I'm widening the gap between me and the person in second place."

Monica looked at her watch. "I gotta run; it's almost noon; I've got calls to make."

We left our half-filled cups of coffee and walked back to the bullpen. We walked out the front door, and *voila!* we switched back to the present with my car just a few feet away. It was that easy.

Back in the car, Darrell said, "Even though it's measurably a lot better, it is still more difficult in this world for women in business, particularly in sales, which has been male-dominated. It's more difficult in your country; it's *really* difficult in my country. This is true with any minority—African-Americans, Asians, gays—you name the minority, it is tougher for them. Make no mistake about it—it *is* more difficult for them. The politicians have passed laws to make it a level playing field, and we like to believe there is a level playing field, but it still isn't. It is still more difficult for women and minorities. Women aren't really a minority in *numbers*, but in certain executive ranks, they are. Some women respond by giving up, which smothers their abilities. Others respond by being artificially aggressive. They try to act tough, be tough. But that act *distorts their abilities*, distorts who they really are. Yes, the Degree of Difficulty was ramped up a few notches for Monica, but you saw her success. Unfortunately, women and minorities have to stay *more* focused—they shouldn't have to—but there is a big benefit of being more focused. You've seen the results with Monica. She's one of the thousands of women who are proving they can make it to the top, that it is indeed possible, even though they have to have more discipline, more focus."

"What was that stuff about lube jobs, oil changes, tune-ups?" I asked. "You lost me there. Were you talking about her car?"

Darrell laughed. "Funny," Darrell said, "now *that's* funny." He laughed some more.

When he was down to the giggling stage, Darrell said, "Let's go."

"Where to?" I asked.

"Golf course," Darrell said. "Where else?"

Chapter 9

Darrell told me which golf course was our destination. On the drive to the golf course, I asked Darrell, "You going to wish yourself some clubs?"

Darrell chuckled, "You'll see."

We were at the golf course in twenty minutes.

I came prepared; I had golf clubs in the trunk of my car. You never knew when you could slip away from work and knock off at least nine holes of golf. I opened the trunk and reached for my clubs.

"Leave them there," Darrell said. "You won't need them."

I wondered if he was going to wish *me* some clubs, maybe some new Pings.

We walked to the pro shop and stepped inside.

"Hey, Darrell, welcome!" The voice was familiar to me.

I looked across the room, and behind the counter was *George!*

Darrell introduced us.

George could see we weren't dressed for a round of golf, so he offered us a cup of coffee. We stepped outside and sat at a table with an umbrella shading us from the sun.

Darrell said to George, "Tell Elmer how you changed from a job that you loved to a job that you love."

George laughed. "That's a good way of putting it," George said.

"Well, it all started during the pandemic," George said. "Remember how it turned everything upside down?"

I nodded, even though it didn't change my life much. Sure, I couldn't go to bars or restaurants for a while, but golf courses were open, and people were buying houses.

"The travel business went into the toilet," George said. "The airline kept me on but reduced my hours. A lot of folks were furloughed. The golf courses, however, boomed. It seemed everybody was playing! So, with my reduced hours at the airport, I was able to put in more time as a starter here at the course."

"But, you're now full-time at the course, as a *manager*, no less," Darrell said. "What's your title again?"

"Rounds Manager," George said. "My job is to fill up the tee-sheet every day with full-pay golfers."

"Even now, long after the pandemic," Darrell said, "you've been able to keep the tee-sheet filled. That's not the case with other golf courses. What did you do differently?"

"It started a long time ago while I was working at the airport," George said. "I'm a big fan of keeping lists. Heck, at the airport, I kept email lists of my favorite passengers, where I would occasionally email them travel tips. Or wish them a Merry Christmas, stuff like that. It was only natural for me to do the same thing when I became a starter at the golf course. I got the email address of every golfer who teed off on my watch. I did this for several years."

"They'd give you their email address?" I asked. "Weren't these golfers afraid of being spammed?"

"Oh, occasionally somebody might be reluctant, but they would be playing with somebody who was already on my list, and that person would say it was okay," George said. "I only infrequently emailed the golfers to give them a heads up when the pro shop had a special on golf balls or a special price for golf on a certain day. No golfer ever asked to be taken off my list. They see it as I am doing them a favor. The golfers appreciate it."

"And so did the owner," Darrell said. "The owner found out what George had been doing and asked him if he could expand it."

"Which, of course, I was able to do," George said. "That led to this job full-time. I really enjoy it. The pay is about equal to what I made at the airport, so I decided on a career change. Now, after work, instead of going home during the summer, I play a quick 9-holes. And, I applied some principles of E-W-E to my golf game, and I'm now playing better than ever before."

Chapter 10

"We gotta go," Darrell said. He bowed to George, and we were off like a race just started.

"Where to?" I asked.

"Your office, pal," Darrell said. "I've taken up enough of your time today. You have to get to work."

As we approached my office building in suburban Beaverton, I noticed the sun was lower than it should be. It should be about noon, but the sun was on the eastern horizon. I looked at my watch. 11:49am. Just as I glanced away from my watch, I noticed the minute hand start to move *backwards*. It started reversing slowly—about one minute per second. Then it picked up steam, and it circled the face of the watch in about ten seconds. My watch had lost an hour in about ten seconds! The next hour was lost in about five seconds. I stared at it, the minute hand flying backwards in a blur, and it came to a stop at 9:31am.

"Neat trick, eh?" Darrell said. "How time flies! Backwards!"

Why should I be surprised? We had walked through mirrors and maintenance closets traversing between time. Now we did it just sitting in my car.

"You'll find this interesting, *really* interesting," Darrell said as he got out of my car. I had parked it in my usual spot in the parking lot behind my office.

We walked inside. You could smell coffee. Several other real estate agents were at their cubicles making phone calls. I mumbled my usual hello as we walked through, but they seemed to be involved in their phone conversations and didn't acknowledge me. As I walked to my cubicle, I saw my boss in his office on the phone. I waved, but he didn't see me. I turned the corner to my cubicle. I stopped abruptly. I was *already* there.

I was already sitting at my desk, reading the sports section of *The Oregonian*.

I turned and looked at Darrell.

"I told you this was going to be really interesting," he said. "I thought you'd like to see what *you* look like at work."

"We're invisible?" I whispered, thinking this was a new angle to this time travel stuff.

He nodded.

"You don't need to whisper," Darrell said. "They can't see you, hear you, or touch you."

I walked over to one of my co-workers. "I've got that twenty dollars I owe you," I said to the salesman in the next cubicle. I waved a twenty-dollar bill out to him as if it was a small flag. He didn't look up. He didn't grab the twenty. That might have been his only chance to get it back. Tough luck for him.

This invisible stuff was fun. I walked over to my boss's office. He was just hanging up the phone. "Hey, Jerry," I said, "before you make another call, let me ask you a question. Were you born a jerk, or did you just grow into one?"

No response.

Darrell came up behind me. "I wouldn't push it," he said. "This time travel isn't an exact science, you know. Sometimes parts of different worlds seep through, at least in a person's memory."

I backed away. Darrell said, "C'mon, let's you and me watch *you*. You might find it interesting."

We walked back to my cubicle.

I don't know what is more tedious—*living* my life or *watching* my life? While others answered phones, writing things on memo pads, looking through listings on their computer, I just sat there reading the paper. My only activity was getting up to refill my coffee.

Finally, the phone rang. I watched myself pick it up. Almost as a reflex action, I saw my feet elevate up to the desk. Yep, that was my usual position, all right. Feet up on my desk while on the phone. A real big-shot.

As if to justify myself to Darrell, I said, "Well, what can I say? It's a boring job."

"More boring than making coffee and serving lemon meringue pie all day?" he asked. "Or punching tickets or making 40 phone calls to prospects before leaving for work?"

I remembered seeing Mack and George and Monica working with so much joy and passion. Then I remembered Mack, George, and Monica before they had met Darrell, seeing them looking like me—bored, sleepy, waiting for something to happen. That was *me* in a nutshell—bored, sleepy, waiting for something to happen. How many *years* would I be waiting for something to happen?

My real life was dull enough but *watching* it was even worse. It was fun watching Mack, George, and Monica when they had that joy and passion for working. And, it had looked like they were having *fun* at work. I guess I never equated *fun* and *work*. Work was something you *had* to do. Sort of like when we were kids, and we *had* to go to school. It wasn't optional. Sure, school, like work, had *elements* of fun. The camaraderie of school was fun. I remember that recess was fun in grade school. Sometimes there was a certain camaraderie at work that was fun. But I equated work to taking a history class. What fun is that?

"How long do we have to watch this?" I asked Darrell.

"Well, we could walk through that closet door and go into your past about five years ago. Would that be any more exciting?"

I physically shuddered. "The only thing that would change would be the date on the newspaper," I said. It's not that I was lazy. I put in at least forty hours a week. Probably closer to fifty hours a week when you consider the weekends showing houses to people who seemed just to want to look. However, I just might be *Exhibit B* on E-W-E—*Effective* Work Ethic. I put in my time—a lot of time—it's just not very *effective*. Instead of E-W-E, Darrell might label my work ethic N-E-W-W-E. Not Effective and Wasted Work Ethic didn't have a very nice ring to it.

Instead of going back about five years, a better idea came to me. "Hey, Darrell, let's take a peek at the future."

"I normally don't go into the future," Darrell said.

"Why not?"

"Don't need to," Darrell said. "You've seen the present with Mack and Monica and George. And, you've seen their past. Is there any doubt that their future will be even more fun and exciting?"

He had a point. Mack, George, and Monica weren't going to lose that joy and passion for work.

"But with you, I'll make an exception," Darrell said. "Wanna go to the future, pal? We'll go to your future. Buckle up."

"Let's go," I said.

"Follow me," Darrell said. He headed for the room that had the copy machine, coffee machine, and reams of paper.

Darrell helped himself to the coffee. "You got any real cream or just this junk?" Darrell asked, pointing to the powdered cream. I told him the powdered stuff was it.

"Any bagels? Donuts?" Darrell asked.

"Nope, you got to bring your own," I said, shrugging my shoulders. Darrell frowned.

"OK, let's go take a look at the future," Darrell said, grumbling as if he had to make the journey on an empty stomach. He walked around me to the office.

I followed him back to my cubicle. I was sitting there reading *The Oregonian* sports section.

"I thought we were going to jump to the future by five years or so," I said.

"We just did," Darrell said, smiling, or it could be a smirk.

I looked at myself reading the newspaper. "You trying to pull a practical joke or something? Nothing has changed. We haven't walked five years into the future."

"Take a look at the newspaper, pal."

I picked up the front section of *The Oregonian*. Damnation! It *was* five years from just a few minutes ago. Nothing else had changed except time. I took a closer look at myself. The 'me' sitting at my cubicle was developing a paunch. A few gray hairs too. And, jeez, my hair was thinning pretty good on the back top of my head. When my future me turned the page of the paper, I noticed that I no longer had a wedding ring on my finger. I glanced over at the corner of my desk. My wife's picture was gone. There was just space where the photo had been. There wasn't a replacement photo of some alluring actress-type who had somehow fallen in love with me.

"What about the wish?" I asked Darrell.

"What about it?"

"I thought that with that one wish things would have changed as it did for Mack and Monica and George," I said. "Heck, this is as boring as five years ago."

"You wished for the wrong thing."

Chapter 11

"*Wished for the wrong thing?*" I practically shouted.
Darrell nodded.
"*How is that possible?*" I demanded. I was hyper. Here's the *one chance*—albeit as illogical as it can be, coming from a genie—to hit The Big One, and *nothing had changed!* It was akin to having the winning Megabucks lottery ticket worth millions safely tucked into my jeans pocket and then throwing those jeans into the clothes washer, obliterating the ticket.
"You were supposed to *guide* me, to *help* me," I said.
"Whoa there," Darrell said, holding up one hand like a traffic cop stopping traffic. "First of all, there is no rule that I have to guide you or help you. I'm like a mailman—I just deliver, I don't write the letter," Darrell said. "You've got a free choice, a free will in this. *The choice is all yours.* You can't blame me for your wish…or, for that matter, your life. But I believe in more personal service, so I have *shown* you Mack—before and after his wish. I have *shown* you Monica—before and after *her* wish. I have *shown* you George, before and after *his* wish. And finally, I have shown you *yourself*—before and after *your* wish. You just didn't pay attention. You just made the wrong wish, pal."
"What did I wish for?"
"You'll find out," Darrell said.
I looked back at myself, reading the paper. I sat down on the spare plastic chair alongside my cubicle. I was just a couple of feet from my future self. This was what I had to look forward to?

Just more of what I had been living? Actually, a little bit *less* than what I had been living. My wife was gone. I don't think she had died—if she had, I probably would have kept her picture on my desk. No, for sure, she left me. Things weren't that terrific between us all the time, but, heck, it wasn't *that bad*. It's not like George Costanza's parents on *Seinfeld*.

"If you could see yourself now," I said to my future self, "you'd put down that stupid paper and do something."

My future self just sat there reading the paper.

"*You're just taking up space!*" I yelled.

My future self just sat there reading the paper. He yawned.

I was about to get up when a man walked over to my future self. It was a guy that I didn't recognize. He had probably been hired within the past five years. He looked to be in his early sixties.

"I got a mailing from Social Security," the man said. "I might be able to pull the trigger and retire at sixty-two. I don't know, though. It's less money. It might be tight."

"Well, if it was me," my future self said, "I'd pull the trigger. I think about retirement every day."

"You do?" the man said, "you're in your early forties. You have twenty years to go."

"Twenty years and counting," my future self said. "I've done some figuring. I think I could live on the Social Security benefits; then it's no more of this crap every day."

"What would you do?" the man said.

"Nothing. Play a little golf, go to a few minor league baseball games, fish. Maybe travel a bit."

"Well, you've got twenty years to think about it."

"Every day, every day," my future self said as if it was some terrific erotic and exotic thought.

I got up out of the plastic chair and walked toward Darrell. I took a look back at my future self. "Idiot," I said and turned to step out of the office.

Darrell joined me outside.

"Where to now?" I asked him. I then noticed that the cars in the parking lot looked different. Not a *lot* different, but the designs of the vehicles were a bit different. Parked in the space where I would typically park my Toyota Camry was a Porsche. Who was the jerk that parked in my parking spot!?

I walked over to it and looked inside. In the tiny back seat, I recognized *my* golf clubs.

The car hadn't been washed in an eon, and there was a ding on the left front fender. Some of the paint had chipped off, and rust had formed.

I turned to Darrell. "This is still five years into the future, isn't it?"

Darrell nodded.

"This Porsche, it's *mine*?"

Darrell nodded.

It gave me hope. Maybe things had turned upwards, perhaps I had wished for the right thing, and this was one of the fruits of my new life. Maybe, *just maybe*, watching my future self was only a brief snapshot that wasn't really indicative of how I lived. Yeah, perhaps I wasn't married anymore, but with this Porsche, maybe I had some beautiful young thing instead.

Then an awful thought struck me.

"*This* isn't what I wished for, is it?" I asked Darrell, pointing at the Porsche.

He nodded.

"*NOOOOOOOOOO!*" I screamed. "I couldn't have been this stupid! Get one wish from a genie, and *I wish for a Porsche?*"

Chapter 12

I was driving now. Not the Porsche, but my Toyota Camry. Darrell was in the passenger seat.

We had re-entered my office, walked by the coffee machine, and then walked out, once again into the parking lot. Crazy, but that's how we time traveled back to the present. Amazing how easy this time travel stuff is if you know the tricks. I could probably write a book on time travel.

I felt like speeding up and driving into a brick wall. How stupid I was! A *Porsche*! Instead of speeding up, I slowed down. I turned into a parking space in front of a seedy-looking bar.

I had never been to this bar before. I had driven by it enough times, but it looked like a low-rent dive bar. We went inside. Darrell probably thought he could get a pizza in there.

Sleazy bar looks better on the outside than on the inside.

    Inside, it was dimly lit. There were four or five guys at the bar. It looked like they were in for the day. There were a few small tables with chairs. These were empty. No eaters here. This was a type of place to just slap down a twenty-dollar bill on the bar and keep drinking until the twenty was gone. Then, perhaps, fish out another twenty-dollar bill and do it again.
    We walked over to an empty corner table and sat down. The waitress took our orders. A 'Scotch on the Rocks' for me. A Diet Coke for Darrell.
    As she was placing the drinks in front of us, I said to the waitress, "I'll have another one of those."
    She nodded. She had seen the type before.
    I slurped down the Scotch like I was drinking Gatorade after playing a round of tennis.
    The waitress was good. The second Scotch was there in a blink. I nodded to her for another. She gave me a slight nod back. Yes, she had seen the type and knew how to provide the quick drinks.
    "All I've ever wanted is to be happy," I said to Darrell. "Just like anybody else, only wanted to be happy."

Darrell took a sip of his Diet Coke.

"You know, Darrell," I said, "there should be classes in how to be happy. They should have taught us that in school. Or at least in college."

"There are classes, so to speak."

"There are?" I asked.

"Sure, there are a lot of self-help books out there."

"I bought some of those books," I said.

"So, what happened?" Darrell asked.

"Nothing. They were mostly general rah-rah stuff. You know, positive mental attitude stuff. Think better of yourself. All that crap. After a while, I just got bored and quit reading. It's easy to say, 'have a positive mental attitude' if you're the one selling millions of dollars' worth of tapes and books about having a positive mental attitude. But like I said, all I've ever wanted is to be happy."

"Is that your wish? To be happy?"

"Yes! That would be everybody's wish, wouldn't it?"

"I can grant you that wish," Darrell said. "To be happy." He fished into his suit pocket and brought out a set of car keys. He tossed them on the table.

The familiar Porsche crest was on the keychain.

"Here's happiness," Darrell said.

I picked up the keys. It surprised me, but I felt a strange surge of power emanating from the keys.

I downed the rest of my Scotch. This stuff wasn't affecting me at all. They must serve watered-down drinks at this joint. I chewed on the ice.

When I think about the Porsche and caress the keys, I do indeed feel a certain power—a peculiar type of happiness. A Porsche was a statement of success, something that I had always been looking for. I thought about how the Porsche could change my life. When I took a customer to look at a house, the customer would certainly be impressed. The customer would think that he was dealing with a highly successful real estate agent. The customer would listen more carefully to what I said. I'd close more deals, that was for sure. More sales would have a positive effect on my wife, too. She'd see a different me. She'd sense that I was more important. She would cheerlead me as I closed deal after deal after deal. Yes, as stupid as I looked back at my office, maybe the Porsche would jump-start me, maybe—just *maybe*—a Porsche was the *right* wish. Yes, this was a promising train of thought.

A moment of clear thinking washed across me. *Wait just a minute!* Am I now making the stupid decision that I had just minutes ago cursed myself for? I was! I was luring myself into taking a Porsche as my wish. Maybe when I had made the decision before, I had been drinking. Wow, these parallel worlds can get confusing. Yes, the Porsche would make me happy. Short-term. Maybe a month. But it wouldn't really *change* anything. I pushed the car keys across the table toward Darrell.

"Those keys would provide me short-term happiness, Darrell," I said, "but I've pursued short-term happiness all my life. I'm an expert on that. I want long-term happiness. I want happiness for the rest of my life."

"That's your 'official' wish?" Darrell asked.

"Yes," I said, almost with a posture of defiance. "*Yes*, that's what my *official* wish is. *I want happiness for the rest of my life*."

"That's your one wish?" Darrell asked again. "You're sure?"

"Yes, yes, yes," I said. "That's it, *pal*." I added the 'pal' to mimic Darrell a little.

"I can do that," Darrell said. "Sure, I can do that."

"Well, what do we do next? Do you zap me or something?"

"I need to give you a warning first," Darrell said.

"Uh-oh, here we go," I said. "More ground rules."

"No, no, it's nothing like that. I just wanted to be able to explain happiness to you. If you had taken those Porsche keys, you would have been happy, right?"

"Right."

"But what happens if you hadn't taken *care* of the car?"

"How so?" I asked.

"You know, oil changes, lube jobs, tune-ups, those types of things. What if you did *none* of those things? The performance of the Porsche would have gotten worse and worse. After a while, you'd be really *unhappy* about that car."

"I wouldn't do that," I said. "That would be stupid. I'd give it oil changes; I'd get it tuned. I'd take care of it."

"Oh, you would, would you?" Darrell said. "If we went back to the parking lot and gave you a test spin of that Porsche with your golf clubs in the back seat, you'd find that your Camry performed much better than your Porsche. You'd find that your Porsche badly needed a tune-up, but you didn't want to spend the hundreds of dollars it cost to get one. What about the left front fender? Yeah, dings will happen. But you saw the rust. That ding has been there for a while. You didn't have it fixed. You're driving a five-year-old car that's closing in on becoming an old piece of junk, pal, and you started with one of the finest cars money can buy. The same thing applies to happiness. If you don't take care of it, if you don't provide the 'oil changes and lube jobs and tune-ups,' then happiness would turn pretty quickly into a clunker."

"So how do you take 'happiness' in for a tune-up?" I asked.

"Well, that's what *you* have to provide to support your wish," Darrell said. "The oil changes, the lube jobs, the tune-ups. You've *already* got the Porsche. The Porsche is *you*. Whether you have thought about it or not, like a Porsche, you're a wonderful machine. Far better than what those German auto guys could have created. That's *you*. You're a wonderful machine.

What you've needed are the oil changes, lube jobs and tune-ups. I can't grant you those. *You* gotta provide them. If you provide them, you'll be just like a finely-tuned race car."

"OK," I said, "I'm getting tired of talking about these analogies—what are those so-called 'oil changes, lube jobs and tune-ups' that I gotta provide? I'm ready."

"Not so fast," Darrell said. "The first step to happiness is that you have to change your thinking a little bit. Not a lot, just a little bit. You'll be able to do it easy."

"What do I have to do?"

"Don't think 'happiness.' Don't even *think* it. Think this: *success in what you do for a living*," Darrell said. "That's the first step and a small one at that. *Think success in what you do for a living*. Happiness is a by-product of being successful."

Darrell held up his hand as if to stop me from talking. You bet I was going to debate what he was saying.

"I know what you're going to say," Darrell said, "that there are a lot of what you consider successful people who really aren't happy. They've got broken marriages. They've got alcohol problems. They got *problems*."

"Right!"

"Let's first take an opposite look at the premise," Darrell said, "I said, 'happiness is a by-product of being successful.' Here's the opposite: *can you be happy if you're not successful?*"

I thought about that for a moment. Can you be happy if you're not successful? I repeated the thought: *Can you be happy if you're not successful?*

Before I could say anything, Darrell said, "For instance, let's say you're a third-grade teacher. You hate your job. You hate the kids you are teaching. You hate the kids' parents. You really don't like many of your fellow teachers. As if it was a great surprise, you're also a lousy teacher. You just couldn't be a great teacher if you hated your job, hated the kids, hated your fellow teachers. Now, and this is important, *could that same third-grade teacher be happy in the other parts of his or her life?* Could that teacher have a satisfying marriage?"

"Probably not," I said and then amended it, "most assuredly not."

"That third-grade teacher would be just as unhappy off the job as on the job. Sure, that teacher might be able to drown his or her unhappiness with TV or some inane hobby or even drinking or drugs, but no matter what, that teacher would be unhappy."

"Look at the reverse. What if that third-grade teacher *loved* the job, *loved* the students, *loved* the challenge, enjoyed the fellow teachers? Most likely, that teacher would be a great teacher—a *fabulous* teacher. And that teacher would be considered successful at what he or she does for a living. My feeling is that third-grade teacher would have a better marriage, be more involved in other parts of his or her life. In short, that teacher would be *happy*."

"How could I argue that? I could throw money into the equation. As we all know, third-grade teachers don't make a fortune. What about money?" I asked.

"That's where people confuse the issue," Darrell said. "Yeah, yeah, yeah, we've all heard that money doesn't buy happiness. Well, let's look at what does buy happiness? If money isn't it, *what does buy happiness*?"

I shrugged my shoulders.

Darrell hunched over the table. He was really into it. He said, "What buys happiness for that third-grade teacher is that they *love their job,* they love their students, they love the challenge of accelerating the progress of their students."

"They have a joy and a passion for their work like Mack and Monica and George," I said.

"That's right. They have *joy* and a *passion* for *what they do for a living*. If they had a little more money, that would be terrific because they'd be able to buy a few more things, but that wouldn't make them any happier. Look at George. George really can't make any more money. But does he seem happy?"

"He sure does. I'd love to feel the way he feels," I said.

"That's what the oil changes, lube jobs and tune-ups do," Darrell said. "Once you start thinking *success at what you do for a living*, then you just need to apply the oil changes, lube jobs and tune-ups. It works automatically, positively, *every time*, no matter if you're a real estate salesperson or a third-grade teacher or an anthropologist or a ticket agent or a farmer or a heart surgeon. It works automatically, positively, every time for everybody. It absolutely, positively cannot fail. You see those stiffs at the bar—it would work automatically, positively, every time for them too."

"Well then, tell me what those oil changes, lube jobs and tune-ups are," I said.

"Not here," Darrell said, "let's get out of this dive." Darrell looked at the check on the corner of the table. He reached into his pocket and dropped a bunch of bills on the table. "My treat," he said and walked out of the bar.

Chapter 13

Darrell took the keys from me. "Designated driver," he said. "I know a place where we can get a great cup of coffee and a great piece of lemon meringue pie. That'll help sober you up."

The drive to Mack's Diner took only about five minutes. Strange, it had only taken a few minutes when we were coming back from the beach—over an hour away from here. The way this time travel stuff was set up, Mack's one diner was more convenient than the thousands of McDonalds.

We walked into the diner. It was full of people. Toward the back, I saw somebody waving at us. It was George; he was dressed as he had just come from the golf course. He was sitting with Monica, the executive of my beloved Portland Trail Blazers. We walked over to their table. In front of each were cups of coffee.

"Join me," George said. We sat down. Mack came over with three cups and a pot of coffee. He set down the cups, poured coffee into each, and put them in front of Darrell and me. The aroma was terrific! Mack then pulled over an empty chair from a nearby table.

"I'm taking a break," Mack said. "Marie will take care of the customers." He then turned to me and said, "Good to see you again, Elmer."

"Go ahead and tell them," Darrell said.

"Tell them what?" I said.

"Tell them that you're ready to make your wish."

"I am?"

"You were about to ten minutes ago," Darrell said. "Remember the Porsche?"

"You were going to choose a *Porsche*?" George asked.

I nodded and then shrugged my shoulders as if that would somehow explain my temporary insanity.

I was saved from sitting there helplessly when Marie delivered three pieces of lemon meringue pie. Great timing!

With a mouth full of lemon meringue pie, I felt I should explain further. "Well, sort of," I said. "I was just *thinking* about it, about a Porsche—I had had a couple of drinks. It wasn't an *official* wish, you know, just a passing thought. Darrell suggested I should instead '*think success in what I do for a living.*'"

"Good advice," Monica said, taking a bite from her piece of pie.

"Yes, excellent advice," Mack said. "By the way, can you taste the difference in the lemons? I had them flown in from Israel today. No—don't worry about that...just enjoy."

"Darrell was going to tell me about oil changes, lube jobs and tune-ups," I said.

George, Monica, and Mack all chuckled as if it was an inside joke.

"He said that oil changes, lube jobs and tune-ups work absolutely, positively every time for everybody, that it is absolutely, positively impossible for them to fail," I said. "Can I ask you guys what was your first oil change?"

"Easy," said Mack, "I cleaned up my kitchen. I steam cleaned it, scrubbed it, washed it, polished it, painted it. I made it look brand new."

"I took some typing lessons," George said. "I went from typing about fifty words a minute to over 90 words a minute. My fingers learned how to fly."

"I took a Dale Carnegie class," Monica said. "You know, where you have to get up in front of strangers and give a little speech."

"Those are *oil changes*?"

"Oil changes in our careers," Mack said. "We had all that crummy oil in the system. The oil change was to improve *something*."

"Improve something? *That's it?*" I asked.

"That's right. Improve *something*! It does sound mundane," Mack said. "On the surface, cleaning the kitchen *sounds* like just a nasty maintenance job. And it was just that. It's something I should have been doing regularly. What was important about it was that it was *part* of something. It wasn't just an isolated cleaning exercise."

"The same with my typing lessons," George said. "On the surface, typing lessons were nice, but I didn't desperately need them. I could type decently. But it was a *part of something*."

"And the same with my attending Dale Carnegie," Monica said. "On the surface, it sounds good that I took the course, although I wasn't a shrinking violet before I took it. But it was a *part of something*."

"What was the something it was part of?" I asked.

"Every ninety days," George said.

"Yep, every ninety days," Mack said.

"Every ninety days," Monica said.

"What do you mean 'every ninety days'"? I asked.

"If you want to '*think success in what you do for a living*,'" Mack said, "*you must* provide the 'oil changes, lube jobs and tune-ups.'"

"Improve or initiate up to three things *every ninety days*," George said.

"That's it?" I asked. "*Improve or initiate up to three things every ninety days?*"

All three nodded their heads.

"That's a little simplistic, isn't it?" I asked.

"Yes, it *sounds* simplistic," Monica said. "But when you think it through, it isn't simplistic at all. You could say that people are improving and initiating something new all the time. That's only partly true. Improving or initiating something new for most people is usually *random* and *infrequent*, and often *unplanned*. What we're talking about is *not random*, it's *not infrequent*, it's *not unplanned*."

"Why just three things?" I asked. "Why not ten?"

"*Up* to three things," George corrected me. "It could be only one thing that you would try to improve or initiate. If I made a list of things to improve or initiate when I first started this, it could have fifteen items. That's too many. I would have been overwhelmed. My actions would become paralyzed. *Up* to three things are not too many; you can focus on fewer things to improve."

"Also, it makes *you* make a decision," Mack said. "*You* have to decide what the three things are. It's not your boss deciding; it's not your spouse deciding; it's not your parents deciding. It's *you*. If *you* are making the decision and choosing up to three things, you find that you have a little more dedication and vigor in improving or initiating. Now you can see how it's planned and not random."

Mack nodded to Marie, the waitress. Since we had all finished our lemon meringue pie, she was bringing over another serving. Usually, I'm not a big fan of desserts. But this pie was the best.

Mack continued. "I'll give you an example of me choosing. My first oil change was to clean the kitchen. That improved something that I do for a living. However, if somebody had *told* me that I *had* to clean up the kitchen, I probably would have done it, but not with the dedication and vigor it took to make it stunningly spotless."

That made sense to me. My boss had stopped trying to suggest areas for me to improve after he had seen how I had either resisted those suggestions or just gone through the motions.

"*You* get to choose what you want to improve," Monica said. "After meeting Darrell, I started to *think* that I could move up the sales ladder at the 76ers. But I lacked a little self-confidence in making that move. I took the Dale Carnegie course just to improve my confidence. If my boss had suggested taking the course, I probably would have thought, *what's with him*?"

"*You* also get to choose *how much* you want to improve or *how far* to take a new project," George said. "*You* set the benchmarks. For instance, when I started taking the typing lessons, I thought I wanted to reach 120 words a minute. Somewhere along the line, *I* found that 90 words a minute was sufficient. After all, I wasn't typing long documents. With what I was typing every day, 90 words a minute had the effect of doubling my efficiency. Reaching 120 words a minute wouldn't have provided any more efficiency. So, what did I do? I stopped taking lessons. I dropped out of that class. If *somebody else* had set my goals, I would have continued on without purpose. I'd probably have gotten bored. I might have even resented it. I wouldn't have been as eager to start improving something else."

That also made sense to me—a lot of sense.

"Yeah, look at my coffee," Mack said. "I just wanted to improve it a bit. It was so awful before."

"You can say that again," Darrell interrupted. He had just been listening, nodding his head.

Mack laughed. "Well, I just wanted to focus on the coffee as one of my three things in ninety days. But then I really got into it. It no longer became something I wanted to improve. It sorta crossed over into the category of initiating something *new*. I spent hours buying exotic coffee beans, experimenting, tasting. This became *fun*. I was initiating something *new*. Each day I could hardly wait to get to the diner to see how my customers liked my new blend."

"That's when I started to notice a joy of work, a passion in Mack," Darrell said. "As you saw for yourself," Darrell said to me, "that joy and passion are unmistakable—it just exudes from him."

"And it doesn't go away," George said, "as long as you're improving or initiating up to three things every ninety days. You see, whether you realize it or not at the time, *you're completely reshaping your job*—no matter what it is—into what *you* want that job to be."

"Yeah," Mack said, "look at George's job at the airport. It was punching tickets. You can't get away from that. But boy, did he have fun. And now he has a whole new set of challenges out at the golf course."

"The reason I have fun at the golf course," George said, "is that I am improving or initiating something new in everything around filling up that tee-sheet at the golf course. I'm shaping that job into *what I want that job to be*."

"Why every ninety days?" I asked.

"It's like a corporation's Quarterly Report," Darrell said, "except we look at it as a Quarterly *Preview*. A corporation's Quarterly Report is basically a report card on how it performed over the previous ninety days. It's after the fact. A Quarterly *Preview* is a conscious, planned effort to look at how to improve over the *next* ninety days. Ninety days is enough time to improve something or to initiate something new. And, there are four ninety-day segments in a year. That's breaking the year up into *bite-size pieces*. Now you've got four Quarterly Previews in each year."

"Think this through for a minute," George said. "Let's say you came up with three things that you wanted to improve or initiate every ninety days. That would be *twelve things* that you initiated or improved in one year! Just think how you would have improved yourself and how your job would have changed! *You would have completely reshaped your job the way you would want it to be.* Sure, the basic function may be the same—like punching tickets was for me—but everything around that job function would have *changed,* changed to your liking. You would have reshaped that job the way you wanted it to be. If you're with a big corporation, your boss will notice your improvement or your boss's boss would notice it. You'd probably get promotions a lot faster—you'd be on a fast track. Take a look at Monica. Once she started making those ticket sales at the 76ers, she was on a real fast track where bosses noticed her improvement."

"Let's look at it more conservatively," Monica said. "What if you could come up with *only one thing* to improve or initiate every ninety days? Just one. That would be four things that you would improve or initiate in one year. Think how those four things could change your job!"

"In two years, you could have improved or initiated eight to twenty-four things," Darrell said. "When you look at it in ninety-day bites, it's not too intimidating."

"In fact, it's pretty easy," Mack said.

"The most difficult part isn't improving or initiating," Monica said. "You'll find that after a while, the most difficult part is the *planning.* Yeah, sure, it's relatively easy to figure out what to improve or initiate in the first few ninety-day segments. For instance, can I ask you, what one thing would you like to improve or initiate over the next ninety days?"

That wasn't a difficult question at all. I took a sip of that wonderful coffee. "Well, one thing I would like to improve," I said, "is to come in earlier to work. Instead of coming in about nine-thirty in the morning, I'd like to come in about eight o'clock. I'd probably be the first one in the office at that time."

"See how easy it was to come up with that first thing?" Monica said. "Now, what's the degree of difficulty to be the first one in the office?"

"It shouldn't be difficult at all," I said, "I get up at five-thirty on Saturdays and Sundays to play golf. If I do it for golf, I can do it to get to work early. I just don't know what I'd do there that early. Except maybe read the paper earlier."

"Don't worry about what you would do if you got there at eight o'clock," Darrell said. "If you decide to improve or initiate something else, you've now created the time for that. In fact, you would have an extra hour and a half a day—or seven and a half hours a week—to work on that other thing to improve or initiate. That's like getting an extra day a week."

"Now, what would you like to improve or initiate once you've found an extra day a week?" George asked.

I took another sip of coffee. I ate another bite of the pie.

"You see," Mack said, "the first thing to improve or initiate came really easy. Now you have to *think*. That's good. Nobody's *telling* you what you gotta do. You're *planning* it."

"Yeah, I like this," I said. "You know, with that extra time, there is one thing I'd like to initiate. I've been thinking about it off and on for a while, but I just kept putting it off."

"What's that?"

"Well, let me bore you a little bit about the residential real estate business," I said. "A key to this business is to get referrals—you know, to get people I know to recommend to friends that are looking to sell their house to use me as the listing agent. If I'm the listing agent, I get fifty percent of the commission no matter who sells the house."

"How many real estate agents are there in the Portland area?" George asked.

"About six thousand," I said.

"Wow, if you were the listing agent," George said, "you'd have potentially six thousand real estate agents trying to sell the house you listed. Yes, I can see where it is important to be the listing agent."

"And, if *I* sell the house that I listed," I said, "I get 100% of the commission. So, I've been thinking about how to increase my listings. People always know *somebody* that is thinking about selling their house. I just have to have them think of *me* when they're thinking of selling their house. But you can't always be bugging your friends, saying, 'Know anybody that wants to sell their house?' After a while, you wouldn't have any friends."

"So, how do you get them to think about you?" Monica asked.

"A greeting card," I said. "Not a birthday card. But a humorous *Listing Card*. In a light, humorous way, I'd send a card out about every…well… ninety days to all my friends and acquaintances. I would send an actual card—not an email. People like getting cards. They'd enjoy mine, and some of them would recommend me to a person who is thinking about selling their house."

"Good idea," George said. "Who makes these cards?"

"There are a bunch of cards out there for real estate agents, but nothing that I like," I said. "I've been thinking about creating my own. I think I could do it on a computer. There's only one problem that's made me procrastinate on it."

"What's that?" Mack asked.

"I don't know how to do graphics on a computer. I just use a computer for emails and games."

"Aha…there's the *second thing* that you can improve or initiate," George said. "You've got an extra hour and a half a day to learn, really learn the computer. With the graphic software programs they have today, you'll learn this lickety-split."

"Right, right," I said. It was like a light bulb had been turned on in my head. "I really hadn't been thinking about it that way."

"OK, that's all," Darrell said. "You've got three things to improve or initiate over the next ninety days. *One*, get into the office at eight o'clock every day. *Two*, take a computer class—either online or at a community college. *Three*, create the first one of those Listing Greeting Cards. Write those three things down. Don't write down any more. Just concentrate on those three. Don't even *think* about what your next three things will be in the ninety days following these ninety days. Just think about the three things for the next ninety days."

"You see how they sorta flow together," Monica said, "if you're thinking about how to be successful in what you do for a living? *One thing just naturally leads to another.* The key is *you* choose how you want to shape your job."

"Not to put a negative spin on this," Darrell said, "but what would be the consequences if the *Listing Greeting Card* thing didn't work out?"

"What do you mean?" I asked.

"Well, what if I just sent out a bunch of cute cards and nothing happened," Darrell said. "What if this idea didn't work at getting any listings?"

"Well," I said, thinking. "I guess I know that I at least gave it a good shot."

"*And*, you made it a habit of being the first one in the office *and* you learned a handy software program," Darrell said. "With that new habit and that new skill, you would be better prepared to improve or initiate things in your *next* ninety days. And, once you're on track to improve or initiate up to three things every ninety days, you'll find that *improvement begets improvement*, that *initiating new things begets initiating new things*."

"You've probably got a better idea of E-W-E—Effective Work Ethic now—don't you?" asked Mack.

"I sure do—improving and initiating up to three things every ninety days," I said. "I'm getting excited. I can see why you guys have so much joy and passion in your jobs. I'm starting to feel more joy and passion for *my* job than ever before, and I haven't even started E-W-E yet!"

I took another sip of the coffee. It was time for me to officially make the wish. "OK, how do I do this—how do I make the wish?" I asked.

Darrell laughed. "Just like when you were a little kid," Darrell said, "except you don't have to close your eyes and blow out any candles. And unlike Dorothy in *The Wizard of Oz*, you don't have to click your heels together three times. Just state your wish."

I cleared my throat a little. "I wish for success in what I do for a living," I said.

There were no lightning bolts. No thunder. No drum roll. No fireworks. It was just like I was talking. Darrell should add some special effects.

"I grant you the wish," Darrell said.

"That's it? That's all there is to it?" I asked.

"That's all there is to it," Darrell said.

"Let him make an amendment to that," Mack said.

Darrell looked at Mack questioningly.

"He should add 'joy and passion' somewhere in that sentence," Mack said.

"That's a qualifying phrase that isn't necessary," Darrell said. "What he wished for, *'I wish for success in what I do for a living'* is ample. If he provides the oil changes, lube jobs and tune-ups, the joy and passion just naturally come. The only way to have joy and passion in work is to improve or initiate things. Once you stop improving or initiating, it gets boring, tedious. I've granted him his wish, and now it's up to him to care for it."

Mack, Monica, and George congratulated me.

"You're going to have the time of your life," Mack said.

"You'll see," George said, "you're going to have so much fun, so much fun." George looked at his watch. "Well, I think I've had my quota of lemon meringue pie, but my wife hasn't. Mack, can I get a piece to go?"

"Sure, George, follow me. I've got to get back to work anyway," Mack said.

"And I've got a meeting to go to," Monica said.

Mack, Monica, and George shook my hand, congratulated me again, and Darrell and I were left alone.

"What's next?" I asked Darrell.

"You go to work tomorrow at eight o'clock; that's what's next," Darrell said.

He got up from the table.

"Oh, there is one more thing," Darrell said. "You've got to insert me in another receptacle. It can't be a spray can. I should've never let that guy put me in there. Geez, the can falls into the ocean, and I gotta travel seven thousand miles. Some of those waves on the Pacific get pretty big, you know. I was tossed around like a ping pong ball in a tornado. Plus, it could have been decades before somebody found me. Think of all those wishes that wouldn't have been made because I was sitting in some spray paint can in the middle of the ocean or on some lonely beach. What a waste that would have been."

"So, how do we do this?" I asked.

"Follow me, pal," Darrell said.

Haven't I always, I thought.

We left the diner, waving at Mack, Monica, and George, and walked across the street. I wasn't familiar with this street. It sure wasn't the road to the Oregon beaches where we had walked into Mack's Diner.

We walked to a 7-11 convenience store. There were three people in line at the front counter. We walked to the back where the soda was located.

"Right here," Darrell said, pointing to the soda machine.

"Right here? How do we do this?"

"Just pick a flavor," Darrell said. "Point to it."

"That's it?"

"That's it," Darrell said. "This will be a lot better than a spray can of paint. Somebody will probably buy this soda bottle today and then I'm on to a new adventure."

"I'll be checking in with you occasionally, just like I do with Mack and George and Monica. Well, my friend, you are now positioned to *ride the right horse*—you. But you gotta ride it. You gotta use the oil changes, lube jobs and tune-ups. You've seen the future if you don't. So, as they used to say in those old cowboy movies, *let's ride!*"

"Now point," he said. "What flavor do you like?"

I pointed to a cola drink. Diet.

In a swoosh and a flash, almost like a mini-tornado, Darrell flew into the 16-ounce bottle of diet soda. The top never popped. Just somehow, someway, Darrell was now in that sealed diet cola bottle.

Wow, those special effect geeks in Hollywood would've been envious of Darrell's move to the soda bottle. Those geeks couldn't have done a better job.

I walked back across the street to my car. I got in, started it, and pulled out onto the road.

As I drove home, I was thinking about the whole experience. It seemed so crazy. So unbelievable. Yes, some things in life are impossible to explain without somebody thinking you're crazy. This, for sure, is definitely one of them. And yet, I had been given this one opportunity to be successful in what I do for a living. And be happy. To have a meaningful marriage. So how crazy is that?

As I drove, a thought made me start to chuckle. The chuckle led to a laugh. I was laughing out loud as I drove. It was the thought of some weary person pulling in to get gas, walking into the 7-11, picking a diet soda bottle and a few snacks and then paying at the counter. Yes, then this unsuspecting person unscrewing the bottle top. And then *vrooooom*, their life will change forever. It's good that person bought a few snacks.

Epilogue

I'm now driving a Porsche. No, I didn't get it by using my wish—this one I earned.

This story—all true, of course—took place about five years ago. I'm just getting around to writing about it. For years, I was afraid of telling anybody about it. You know, I didn't want anybody to think I was crazy or something. Now that I'm earning my way, I feel a little more confident talking about my meetings with my genie, Darrell.

You see, I'm doing pretty good right now. Well, a lot better than pretty good. Really good. Really, really good. The oil changes, lube jobs and tune-ups worked like magic. In fact, it's gotten to the point where I can hardly wait for the next ninety days to see what three things I'm going to improve or initiate.

I've got my own real estate brokerage now. The main office is in Portland, Oregon. I've got nine branch offices in four states. One of those branch offices is in Maui, Hawaii. That's where I am now. I'm dictating this while driving from my office to meet my wife at a beautiful seaside restaurant near our beachfront home. Same wife. Terrific woman. It seems that whatever speed bumps we were encountering, we've smoothed down in ninety-day increments.

As you can guess, my lone wish— my wish for success in what I do for a living—came true. Sure, the wish was the easy part. The hard part was the thinking part in the Quarterly Previews. And it wasn't always easy doing the oil changes, lube jobs and tune-ups. But, as Darrell said, *improvement begets improvement, initiating new things begets initiating new things.* Right from the start, I could feel joy and passion in my job, a job that I had hated before I met Darrell.

Once I started my own business, I used the principles I learned from Darrell, Mack, Monica, and George and introduced them to my first employee. She loved it! I hired her as a secretary/receptionist; she is now the Chief Operating Officer. I applied those same principles to my second employee. He loved it. He's now president of our Hawaii operations.

Since it worked so well with me and then with my first two employees, we decided to make E-W-E a standard with any new employee. I look at it this way: if each employee improves a little bit in ninety days, our company will grow in geometric dimension.

As I drive to meet my wife at our favorite beachfront restaurant, I notice another Mack's Diner.

I stop there almost every day when I'm on Maui. This is the first one on Maui and third one on Hawaii. You might have read in THE WALL STREET JOURNAL that he took his company public.

I, of course, bought a nice chunk of the initial stock. How could I pass that up? He instilled that same joy and passion in his employees. The stock was a smash hit, making Mack worth well over fifty million dollars.

I see George all the time at the golf course. Interestingly, some of his former Japanese travelers now come to Portland to play a few rounds of golf with George. He told me he could take early retirement but was having too much fun doing what he does for a living. This weekend, George and his wife are taking a vacation to Maui. We're playing golf on Saturday.

Monica moved on from the Trail Blazers and is the owner of three minor league baseball teams. The teams, not coincidentally, are the best run teams in baseball. Her equity in those teams has made her very rich and a bit famous. In one year, as the top woman in the sports business, she made the 'hat trick'—she made the covers of *Fast Company, Entrepreneur* and *Forbes*. I see her about once a year. She's having so much fun.

As for Darrell, you're probably not the person who walked up to that 7-11 and bought a bottle of diet cola and wound up with that big, fantastic genie. After all, what're the odds of that?

No telling where Darrell can be found now. I see him from time to time, but you never know when he's going to show up. So, if you'd like to get one wish granted, I've got an idea that might interest you. Darrell appointed me as his surrogate, and I—yes, *me*—could grant you your one wish.

Being a 'surrogate Darrell' is pretty easy for me. I don't even have to eat four cheeseburgers at a time or walk through mirrors. I just have to tell you one thing.

But, before I will grant you your wish, *you* have to do just one thing. And you have to do it before you close this book. If you do this one thing, your wish will automatically come true—like Darrell said, *automatically, positively, every time, for everybody*.

That one thing you have to do is to commit right now to provide the oil changes, lube jobs and tune-ups. Commit *right now*, not tomorrow, not next week.

Your commitment starts by checking one of the boxes below.

☐   **Yes**, *I'm going to write something in the spaces for oil changes, lube jobs and tune-ups before I close this book. (If you check this box, your wish will come true.)*

☐   **No**, *I'm going to write something in those spaces another time. (If you check this box, you have significantly increased the degree of difficulty of having your wish come true. Don't let this happen! If you did check this box, erase the checkmark. Check the Yes box. Right now! Believe me, it's so much more fun.)*

If you checked the Yes box, let's proceed.
Read the sentence below out loud.

> **I wish for success in what I do for a living.**

Go ahead, say it ***out loud***.
I grant you your wish.
That's right, your wish has been granted. Sorry, I'm not into special effects, but you'll receive success in whatever you do for a living. That's done.

Now, let's think about oil changes, lube jobs and tune-ups. Remember your commitment when you checked the Yes box.

I'm not going to dictate what your oil changes, lube jobs and tune-ups should be. That is up to you.

Make a list of up to three things you want to improve or initiate over the next ninety days.

Go ahead, think about it for a minute or two and write at least one of them down right now.

1._____
2._____
3._____

Now that you've listed at least one thing, ***let's ride!*** You sure are going to have some fun.

So, is it unfair to use an unfair advantage to get an approval from your boss? Of course not. In this case, an unfair advantage is a fair advantage. *Your* advantage.

Here it is, your advantage. Go ahead, use it, run with it.

Author's Afterword

Jon Spoelstra
findjon@msn.com

I'm back.

Years ago, I was thumbing through a magazine in some lobby waiting for a meeting and read a story about Greek Mythology. In this story, 'opportunity' was represented as a horse. A horse with wings. It could fly! Its name was *Pegasus*.

The Horse of Opportunity

A few days later, I thought about that story. How could I mount this Horse of Opportunity? If I grabbed the horse's wings as it approached, I might have a chance to hoist myself onto the horse's back. However, if I didn't act quick enough and the horse passed, there would be nothing to grab except the tail, and the mental picture of that wasn't appealing. I guess that could be called Opportunity Lost.

The Horse of Opportunity could, of course, represent different things to different people. It could mean a particular job or money or even peace of mind or a special relationship with another person. But *seeing* the opportunity in *advance* is the tricky part. Remember, lunging after opportunity passes doesn't bode well.

I know there have been times when I didn't even see the Horse of Opportunity coming. It happened like this: Opportunity just rode by; I didn't even see it; all I heard was the whoosh. Heck, sometimes I was so unaware I didn't even hear the whoosh.

I've known people who are reluctant or even afraid to jump on the Horse of Opportunity because they are unsure where the ride will take them. I can understand that. Sometimes it might just seem to be too risky.

There must be a better way to prepare for when that Horse of Opportunity comes galloping along. There is. I think the best way is not to lunge at the Horse of Opportunity. Instead, take a single step toward the horse.

That single first step is doing the 90-day preview. Easy. No risk. See what happens.

I've been doing the 90-day preview for most of my adult life and have found that the Horse of Opportunity often *finds* me. I haven't needed to take a flying leap onto that horse because my Quarterly Preview so well prepared me that the Horse of Opportunity sauntered over, knelt, and I easily climbed on.

Now, I see that Horse of Opportunity is coming near.

The Horse of Opportunity is walking right at *you*.

How can I see that with you being where you are and me being where I am? Well, by just reading the *Pigs That Fly Hack*, you've stirred up that Horse of Opportunity. Yup, the Horse of Opportunity is indeed slowly heading in your direction!

Here's what to do immediately: Think of up to three things you would like to improve or initiate in the next 90 days. One thing will suffice. Write them down. Don't just think them; *write them down*. The rest will take care of itself.

Do it now. And then get ready for the ride of your life on the Horse of Opportunity. You'll have fun.

YOUR FIRST QUARTERLY PREVIEW

Start date: Day_____ Date _____
90 Days later: Day_____ Date _____

Up to 3 things to improve or initiate

	Description	Benchmark
1		
2		
3		

For some of your ideas, you'll need approval from a boss, spouse, partner or *somebody*. Getting that approval can be intimidating. It doesn't have to be. For years, I have use what I call The Outrageous Approval Tool. I explain how to use that tool in the second book of my Ideas books. Here's a brief excerpt from *Get Your Ideas Approved*.

There's one question asked of me more than any other during the Q&A at any one of my speeches.

"What *one thing* is most responsible for your successes?"

Yes, I have had some marketing successes, and I've written about those successes in *Marketing Outrageously*, *Marketing Outrageously Redux* **and** *Ice to the Eskimos*.

This book is about the one thing most responsible for my successes: How I have been able to get my bosses to approve anything and everything I wanted to initiate.

My approval percentage is 100%. That includes the really wacky stuff.

I got bosses of all types to approve things. I'm talking about tough bosses, cunning bosses, brilliant bosses, bosses who hated me, bosses who didn't want to approve anything I did, bosses who loved me, government bosses, and even wonderful bosses.

THE FIRST TIME

The first time I got my boss to approve something important that I wanted to initiate, I didn't think it was a career enhancer.

No, my thoughts weren't that lofty; I was just pleased I had the go-sign to bring my idea to life.

It wasn't until a year or so later that I realized I used a tool—yes, an actual *tool*—that I could use as frequently as I wanted to get my boss(es) to approve anything I wanted to do.

I'm not talking about trivial stuff to get approved. I'm talking about ideas that could appear risky—some may even say *ridiculously* dangerous to a career.

I'm not sure of the danger, but I'll grant you that these ideas were *different*. Being different could scare some folks from even *thinking* about asking the boss for approval unless they had what I now call **The Outrageous Approval Tool**. Having that Tool is a game-changer.

Throughout my career, I used The Outrageous Approval Tool, which *never* failed me. You see, some things in life are just not fair, and using The Outrageous Approval Tool is not fair to your boss. You'll get the approval every time. You just have to use it.

Get Your Ideas Approved is not a book about negotiations.

With negotiations, there's often give-and-take. There are compromises. There's settling on a middle ground.

None of those are applicable in this book.

This book is about getting *your idea* approved by *your boss*; about getting your idea approved the way *you* want to make it work.

This book is the proven blueprint on how to get the approval you need and want without taking a risk.

It really is your *unfair advantage* in getting your boss to approve whatever you want to initiate.

So, I then ask the question: is it unfair to use an unfair advantage to get an approval from your boss? My answer: of course not. In this case, an unfair advantage is a fair advantage. *Your* advantage.

Here it is, your advantage. Go ahead, use it, run with it. You and your boss will be delighted that you did.

Dedication

This book is dedicated to those dedicated to making ideas work. I'm talking about Roy Williams, Ray Bard, Joe Sugarman, Howie Nuchow, Steve Pettise, Steve DeLay, my sister Ann Kimberly of indomitable spirit, my son Erik Spoelstra, my daughter Monica Metz and, of course, my wife Lisa, who always has cherished pigs that fly. I can only hope that my grandkids—Alonzo, Santiago and Dante—follow the wisdom of Darrell, our friendly genie.

Books by Jon Spoelstra

Non-Fiction

- **Get Your Ideas Approved**. *Ideas Series #2: Approval.* The art of getting your ideas green-lit even from the toughest, meanest, jerkiest, rudest bosses. And, from the weakest, laziest and wimpiest too.
- **Marketing Outrageously Redux**. *How to increase your revenue by staggering amounts.*
- **Marketing Outrageously**. *Wall Street Journal bestseller.*
- **Ice to the Eskimos**. *How to market a product nobody wants.*

Fiction

- **Do-Overs**. *A Time Travel Thriller of Sudden Second Chances.*
- **Red Chaser**. *A noir thriller of the 1950s, the cold war and the Brooklyn Dodgers.*
- **Who's Killing All My Old Girlfriends?** *Old Guys Murder Mystery #1.*
- **Who's Killing the Fountain of Youth?** *Old guys murder mystery #2.*
- **Who's Killing All the Old Bank Robbers?** *Old Guys Murder Mystery #3*

www.ingramcontent.com/pod-product-compliance
Lightning Source LLC
Chambersburg PA
CBHW070652220526
45466CB00001B/406